Sir Aubrey

Sir Aubrey

A biography of C. Aubrey Smith
England cricketer, West End actor, Hollywood film star

by

DAVID RAYVERN ALLEN

ELM TREE BOOKS
London

First published in Great Britain 1982 by
Elm Tree Books/Hamish Hamilton Ltd
Garden House 57-59 Long Acre London WC2E 9JZ

British Library Cataloguing in Publication Data

Allen, David Rayvern
  Sir Aubrey.
  1. Smith, C. Aubrey 2. Moving-picture actors and
  actresses—Great Britain—Biography
  I. Title
  791.43′028′0924   PN2598.S/
  ISBN 0-241-10590-0

Typeset by Saildean Ltd, Surrey
Printed and bound in Great Britain
at the Pitman Press, Bath

For
BENNY
who
was
kind
enough
to
drop
the
catch!

Contents

Acknowledgements

Sir Aubrey's name worked a magic spell; an instant smile, a ready response, and a great desire to assist in any way possible. The essence of the man was apparent immediately; more than words would be able to evaluate, and volumes could ever speak. The reaction said it all, and this book is an attempt to recreate that feeling.

Firstly, I would like to record my deepest gratitude to Honor Cobb, Aubrey's daughter, without whom this book would have been immeasurably poorer and half the size. A constant stream of anecdote in a historical perspective was only part of her unsparing assistance; letters, photographs, her own scrapbooks – the list is endless and so was her patience.

Aubrey's niece, Diana Wood, as she was when acting as his secretary in the nineteen thirties, now Diana St Clair-Tisdall, gave a remarkably articulate and coherent account of events at that time which proved immensely valuable, for which my heartfelt thanks.

Richard Bradley, Headmaster of Ridley College, St Catherine's, Ontario, ungrudgingly made Aubrey's scrapbooks available for perusal; David Niven took the time to tell of episodes experienced at first hand on the film sets while in transit from France to the West Indies; and Dennis Castle kindly relayed with enchanting humour from the South Coast a multitude of ideas and information on the thespian years. They each provided riches, and mere thanks are poor reward.

'Bunty' Ireland miraculously deciphered my hieroglyphics, and the people below deserve a special accolade for help of various kinds, all beyond the call of any duty.

Staff at the Academy of Motion Picture Arts and Sciences, Los Angeles; Frank Acevedo; G.O. 'Gubby' Allen; R.L. Arrowsmith; Staff at the BBC Reference Library; S. Benjamin; Sir Donald Bradman; E.K. 'Ted' Brown; Robert Brooke; N.C. Buck at St John's College Library, Cambridge; Christopher

Cobb; James D. Coldham; Adrian M. Cole; Alistair Cooke; Ted Du Domaine; Douglas Fairbanks Jnr.; Dr Fernandez-Armisto and his helpers at Charterhouse; David Frith; Thomas Freebairn-Smith; John Gilroy; Benny Green; Stephen Green; the Green Room Club Committee; Edward Grayson; Leslie Gutteridge; John Hayward; Bert Hoyland; Susan Huxley at the British Film Institute; Ursula Kenny; David Kynaston; Patricia Kinnell; Milt Larsen; Professor R.A. Lyttleton; Roger Mann; Rose Marder; Raymond Massey; J.W. McKenzie; Jane Mercer; Clifford Mollison; Robert Montgomery; Louise Musgrave; Brian O'Gorman; Laurence Olivier; H. 'Ossie' Osborne; J. Edmund Peckover; Clive Porter, who found most of the scores; Patricia Roberts; Don Rowan; E. Rotan Sargent; Dr Clifford Severn; George Sidney; Brian Souter; Bill Sullivan; E.W. Swanton; Roy Tisdall; Ben Travers; the Theatre Section Staff of the Victoria and Albert Museum; Eugene Walsh; Mark Wanamaker; E.G. Willett; A.E. Winder; Jean Wong; Alexander Wood; Sue Woodman; Ian Wright; and Leslie Youngren.

For kindly allowing the use of photographs, I am again indebted above all to Honor Cobb, but also to Russell Birdwell of Selznick International Pictures; N.C. Buck of St John's College, Cambridge; Dr Fernandez-Armisto of Charterhouse; Thomas Freebairn-Smith; the Hollywood Cricket Club; Roger Mann; the National Film Archive/Stills Library; David Niven; and the Theatre Department of the Victoria and Albert Museum.

Introduction

'If Sir Aubrey Smith could have joined the company of King Arthur, he would have introduced cricket and become captain of Camelot, for none has shown better how to play both on and off the field.'

Thus spake Crusoe, alias cricket humorist and fellow Carthusian R.C. Robertson-Glasgow. For once Crusoe did not speak entirely with tongue in cheek, for Sir Aubrey was an outstanding example of a race that is practically extinct. The perfect English gentleman has always been an easy target for the cartoonist's caricature, the stage ape and the party impression, and yet the response is invariably an affectionate one – the chuckle is accompanied by a patriotic tingle, perhaps a secret admiration and longing for principles largely lost that formed part of an ethical code showing how to live.

Sir Aubrey Smith was an imposing figure. He was a commanding six feet two and a half inches in height, and his jutting chin and bushy eyebrows framed an uncompromising stare from piercing blue eyes. The size and breadth of his achievement over a period of seventy years defies the imagination. In these days of specialisation it is hard to imagine anyone achieving excellence and eminence in sport, on the stage *and* in films. Yet here was a man who, during a long lifetime, rubbed shoulders with the legendary figures in all three spheres, and whose adventures and accomplishments spread even further than that.

He had been part of the last serious amateur challenge in the F. A. Cup; as a bowler in his 'Round the Corner' days for Cambridge and Sussex, he had troubled and toppled the best batting defences, and been the inspirational force behind a number of historic victories; he had captained the Shaw and Shrewsbury side to Australia, and then led the pioneer English cricket team to South Africa, a highly successful tour which formed a basis for the development of the game in the Union. He had remained in South Africa during the time of the Gold Rush, and had ranched, shared some broking, gone broke, starved and been critically ill. After reading his own obituary in a newspaper, he recovered, returned to England and then stepped on to the stage in some seventy plays.

Sir Charles Hawtrey, Sir Henry Irving, Forbes Robertson, Ellen Terry, Billie Burke, Ethel Barrymore and Mrs Patrick Campbell were a few of the many renowned 'rogues and vagabonds' who played opposite his bristling colonel, cunning politician, distinguished diplomat, well-meaning member of the cloth, mystified physician, wronged husband or simply, fellow of the squirearchy. Aubrey made each character his own, and enveloped each part with an authority to match. Usually, it was a benign authority – '... with a less magnanimous leading man, the production would have been impossible. We were neither of us born to keep the lid on hell!' read George Bernard Shaw's revelatory epistle to Professor Higgins during the revival of *Pygmalion* in 1920, when Mrs Pat's Eliza was proving especially difficult to handle.

Aubrey's 'silent' career in films commenced at the time his employer was sinking with the *Lusitania*, and he once confided to a friendly baronet that he was 'down and out in New York at the age of sixty'.

His movie career found fresh impetus with 'the talkies', when he appeared in over a hundred films portraying exactly the rôle that fitted the American conception of their ancient cousins across the sea. It started with the transfer to the screen of his huge stage success in *The Bachelor Father*, and continued over the next decade and a half, when he worked for every major studio in the film capital. He appeared with some of the greatest stars of the period, in *Queen Christina* with Garbo, *Rebecca* with Olivier and Joan Fontaine, *Dr Jekyll and Mr Hyde* with Spencer Tracy and Ingrid Bergman and for most movie-buffs the definitive version of Anthony Hope's *The Prisoner of Zenda* (alongside Colman, Fairbanks and Niven), when as Colonel Zapt he capped the classic with the immortal line that would have been so appropriate if attributed to him personally: 'Englishman, you are the finest Elphberg of them all'.

Never for a moment during his acting career did Aubrey

forsake his passionate association with cricket. At the turn of the century he had been instrumental in forming a theatrical side called the Thespids, and many a hale and less than hearty thespian from a West End dressing-room was surprised to find himself dressed in virginal white on an open-air stage remote from the purlieus of Piccadilly. Years later, a clause written into one of his film contracts stipulated that he be allowed time off to watch test matches.

Aubrey's arrival in Hollywood in the 1930s heralded a cricketing crusade across California, when he helped found the Hollywood Cricket Club and made it the social centre of the British Film Colony. Boris Karloff, Nigel Bruce, H. B. Warner, Errol Flynn, Basil Rathbone and David Niven performed their strokes on Sunday afternoons, and occasionally Merle Oberon, Olivia de Havilland, Greer Garson and Gladys Cooper went along to watch and make the tea. Well, perhaps not quite tea ...

In 1944, at the age of 81, Aubrey was knighted for services to Anglo-American amity. During the Second World War he had been intensely involved in fund-raising for the Forces, and it would be hard to find an expatriate serviceman who left his door empty-handed.

Once, while toasting Field Marshal Montgomery, Samuel Goldwyn referred to 'the town of our Lady, Queen of the Angels', and more specifically to Hollywood as 'a far-flung outpost of civilization'. For the ever-expanding British community who had made it their home, Aubrey was undoubtedly titular head. A head whose forbidding exterior failed to hide the expansive and warm-hearted generosity within. His unofficial ambassadorial status was confirmed when a British Consul arrived in Los Angeles only to say, 'My job has already been done.' Few would deny that the conferring of a knighthood by the king was long overdue. Yet in a strange way it was not needed. For most who had met him, and millions who had not, he always had been *Sir* Aubrey.

1/Early Years

Fanfare

Announcer (Ben Carpenter): Command Performance USA. The greatest entertainers in America, as requested by you, the servicemen and women of the United States Armed Forces throughout the world. Command Performance presented this week, and every week till it's all there, over there—

(Music: Over There)

Announcer (over music): OK there gang, time to gather round your international walkie talkie and gather another mittful of stardust coming to you in answer to your requests to Command Performance, Armed Forces Radio, Los Angeles, USA. Roll call tonight sounds like we might have borrowed it from the guest list of wayside inns around Sussex, Wessex and Essex. You'll meet such luminaries of greasepaint, cinema and wireless as Sir Aubrey Smith, Dame May Whitty, Reggie Gardner, Ida Lupino, Cary Grant, Jenny Sims, and your Master of Ceremonies, Ronald Colman.

(Applause)

Ronald Colman: Thank you, Ben Carpenter, and greetings from the USA. Command Performance Headquarters has gathered the teabag battalion around the microphone to transplant a bit of Piccadilly to the heart of Hollywood and Vine... So, two of the grandest people I've ever had the pleasure of knowing – Dame May Whitty and Sir Aubrey Smith.

Dame May: Thank you, Ronnie.

Sir Aubrey: You're very kind.

Ronald Colman: And it's most fitting that you should be here because I'm certain that nobody represents the very essence of Britain to American movie goers as you two do.

1

Dame May: Well, maybe that's because we've become a little less Americanised than others of the English colony here. Er, Ronnie, you know, we're rather set in our ways.

Sir Aubrey: After all, at our age what can you expect?

Dame May: Speak for yourself, Aubrey!

Sir Aubrey: Oh.

(Laughter)

Ronald Colman: In other words then, because you are so steeped in the law and tradition of England, America has not yet left its imprint on you. Correct, Sir Aubrey?

Sir Aubrey (in American accent): You ain't just beatin' your chops Jack!

(Laughter)

Ronald Colman: I'm not?

Dame May: No, you're undoubtedly cooking with gas.

(Laughter)

Ronald Colman: This is amazing!

Dame May: Now now Ronnie, let's not blow our top.

(Laughter)

Ronald Colman: Oh, I never thought I'd hear that kind of talk from either of you, no matter how long you'd been in the country. You've always thought no meal was complete without Yorkshire pudding.

Sir Aubrey: Oh, we still insist on Yorkshire pudding with every meal, old boy.

Dame May: Yes … *pause* … only now we dunk it.

(Laughter)

Ronald Colman: Well, I'm glad to see you're both still British down to your fingertips.

Sir Aubrey: 'Course we are, Ronnie, after all England's our home land. The land of our youth.

Ronald Colman: And quite a gay youth it was according to certain rumours which have reached me, Sir Aubrey …

It was towards the end of the Second World War; Sir

Aubrey was in his eighty-first year. As he left the studio to sink into his comfortable limousine for the drive back up Sunset in the direction of his Beverly Hills home, he could not help thinking of that scripted throwaway remark of Ronnie's. It was not really a gay youth. Certainly it had been eventful ...

C. Aubrey Smith was born on the 21st of July 1863, in the City of London. On that day the burlesque *I Am All There Tonight* at the Royal Strand Theatre was causing a few ribs to ache on the morrow, even if some of the audience had not found it all that funny, and a new edition of *The Cricket Bat; and how to use it* by another artist, schoolmaster, musician, actor, cricketer, 'Felix', or Nicholas Wanostrocht to give him his proper name, had just reached the bookstalls. The squawking infant, soon to be christened Charles Aubrey, was delivered in St Stephen's Hospital, Coleman Street, literally just round the corner from the Church of St Mary-le-Bow, which gave him full Cockney status, and also a street or so away from Number 9, Finsbury Place South, where his parents had lodgings at the house of a dentist named Mr Tibbs.

The Smiths were in their mid-twenties, and both had stock connections with vintnery. Aubrey's mother, Sarah Ann, was the only daughter of John Clode, a wine merchant and auctioneer in Windsor, Berkshire, who followed the Clode tradition of serving on the Council and had been Mayor of the town; his father, Charles John, was the third of thirteen children in a family that formed half of Smith and Tyer, a firm of wine merchants based near the Tower of London.

Aubrey, however, was not destined to make his youthful forays among City streets: soon after his arrival his parents moved to Chipping Campden, Gloucestershire, where his father, who had trained as a surgeon, joined a general practice as a doctor at what is now the Cotswold House Hotel. The hotel, where the young Aubrey took his first steps, now boasts an Aubrey Smith Room.

As he grew older, Aubrey found to his cost that his father treated him in exactly the same way as he himself had been treated when young. Charles John had had a conventionally strict Victorian upbringing with a pater who frequently warmed the behinds of his sons, and who expected in turn that his morning paper be warmed by the smoothing irons of his daughters. C. J. had even received a hiding for riding a donkey on a Sunday, and it has to be supposed that the rituals for observing the Lord's Day clouded the fact that the gentle Jesus had done the very same thing.

Now it was Aubrey's turn, and as a child he suffered a number of times at the hands of Charles John. The doctor, who to the outside world seemed charming and gallant, had a streak of cruelty in his nature that stayed with him throughout his life: both Aubrey's daughter Honor and his niece Diana relate instances of an unpleasant nature, which are hard to understand, let alone condone. On one occasion, when he was in his eighties, Charles John asked Diana to look directly into his eyes, whereupon he deliberately burned the back of her hand with his cigarette.

Aubrey always had a deep affection for his mother, although on the surface she might have appeared less likeable than her sophisticated husband. Sarah Ann had a certain obstinacy, and very little sense of humour. She was pedantic with speech: *half*-penny, and *know*-ledge were delivered with old-fashioned pronunciation, and she was quick to correct those who erred; but though her horizons were limited to piano playing, shopping and sewing for the household, her love for her three children – Aubrey and his sisters Beryl and Myrtle – was ever-apparent. But it did not stop her taking a firm line regarding young Aubrey's attitude towards churchgoing. Her son's view was that, as Sunday was a day off, it really did not matter what one wore when attending the Lord's House. His mother insisted he wear his best clothes, to which Aubrey retorted that in that case he would not go at all! This unoriginal childhood conflict left Aubrey with a lifelong aversion to the sound of church bells.

Mind you, it was from his mother that Aubrey enjoyed learning about the family history. His father had attended the Blue Coat School which was then still in London, and after deciding on a career in medicine had performed extremely well in his surgeon's studies at St Thomas's Hospital. He studied at the time when surgery in the operating theatre took place with the surgeons dressed in morning coats, which they occasionally took off if the day were hot or the operation likely to be lengthy. Coats and top hats were then hung on rails at the back of the room, and only very serious cases warranted a rolling up of the sleeves. But the early promise was not fulfilled; a tendency towards self-indulgence allowed Charles John to settle for a less demanding rôle as a G.P. and though years later he was chosen to go on an expedition to Egypt with the Royal Geographical Society, he was not called upon to display skills of a surgical nature.

Charles John, or Charlie-Johnnie as the family later called him, had met his Sarah Ann when attending her father. The dashing young doctor with his easy charm and ready wit captivated the rather shy, thoroughly domesticated young girl who had been taught to play the piano rather well by a tutor of Queen Victoria's. Her parents, however, were less enthralled, and after the two lovers had eloped to get married they observed the 'less than a penny' tradition in such cases by having little to do with her at no cost.

While Aubrey was going to the local school in Chipping Campden, his father was busy 'cutting a dash' on rather a grander scale than his income permitted. His busy social life included joining the Volunteers, riding in competitions for six-in-hand, and taking part in the athletic sports of the North Cotswold Rifle Corps. In 1866 he had won a shooting competition and with it a silver plate biscuit box, and then the following year a 120 yards handicap and 220 yards all comers race, the prizes for which were handsome cups.

The trophies did not help with the bills, however, and so in order to stay solvent the Smiths took in children whose parents were abroad and others who were mentally retarded. This enlarged household needed a lot of looking after, so they hired staff at the local Annual Mop Fair where each worker wanting employment stood with the badge of their office. At the fair there could be found a coachman with his whip, and also a housemaid with her duster. Each would be given one year's contract which only became binding after the 'Little Mop' or 'Runaway Fair' held a few weeks later. The Runaway Fair was the opportunity for either the employer or employee to terminate the engagement if they so wished. Even though the Smith would have been considered only moderately well-to-do, they still managed to take on two indoor maids, a cook, a coachman and a gardener.

The doctor's quick intelligence was obviously not stimulated sufficiently by the aches and pains that surfaced daily in the waiting-room, and he sought to relieve his boredom in other ways. He found that his six-foot one-inch figure, good looks, dark hair and blue eyes were no hindrance when it came to socialising. Apparently the ladies fell like ripe apples, and this sometimes led to a rapid change of practice.

The Smiths moved to Brighton around 1870, and it is easy to see that 'the centre of fashion and provincial capital of social life' would have been an especially attractive environment for Dr Smith. Aubrey was sent to school at the Crescent House Academy on the Marine Parade, Kemp Town. Here, thanks to the enthusiasm of his new headmaster, he was introduced to the rudiments of cricket. For many years, Mr William Adams was Honorary Secretary of the Queen's Club in Brighton, and he took young Aubrey under his wing. The grounding on a gravel wicket taught him to bowl straight, and the advantages of this were to be realised first in the years to come at Charterhouse.

Education at a leading public school was relatively no cheaper then than it is today, and a brother of Aubrey's father, now head of the family wine business, promised to help financially. Indeed, he had provided support at other times when Charles John's extravagances had caused the family purse strings to hang by precarious threads. Fred was a favourite uncle, a big jolly man with a laugh that went on for a very long time, rather like bath water running away, almost a Biblical allusion for someone in the wine trade. Uncle Fred was to finance Aubrey's education through Charterhouse and Cambridge.

Meanwhile, Aubrey's mother had started painstakingly putting together a sailor's suit for her son to wear on his first day at his new school.

Appropriately enough, Aubrey arrived at Charterhouse at the start of the Cricket Quarter in 1875. It was three years since the school had moved from Smithfield in London to Godalming in Surrey, and the number of boys had nearly trebled in that time to just over four hundred.

Charterhouse was then under the stern but fatherly head-mastership of the Rev. Canon W. Haig Brown, and during his long period in office a number of humanising innovations were made. Could it be that the warmth of the undulating Surrey countryside had had a mellowing effect on some of the more barbarous habits of an old English public school system?

For instance, in 1874, the year before Aubrey's arrival, an incident resulting in the mass punishment of a form by Monitors had led to the introduction of a Code of Monitorial Discipline which placed restrictions on the use and application of corporal punishment.

Then, four years later, there was the abolition of the Lemon Peel Fight. The Shrove Tuesday battle, which involved every boy in the school, had for many years been confined to the genteel use of lemon peel as a missile, and the occasion had been aptly described as 'pure citronomachia'. More recently, however, the half lemons had been filled with pebbles and ink which had inflicted considerable injury, so the sixth form declared the practice obsolete.

There had also been wide-spread persecution and bullying of new boys, and this had been stamped on severely when it reached official ears, though unfortunately it provided no safeguard for Aubrey on his first day. The carefully-sewn sailor suit which had taken his mother so long to make attracted a lot of attention and derision from some of the other 'scholars'. They set on young Aubrey and, though he defended desperately, tore the suit from his back. The result of the fracas was bruises all round, and a black eye for Aubrey. That night in the dormitory he cried himself to sleep, not in self-pity for his own hurt, but rather at the thought of his mother and her countless hours of work that now lay in tattered shreds.

Aubrey's entry house at Charterhouse was Uskites, a temporary residence situated at the bottom of the hill on the school side of the River Wey. It was so called because L. M. Stewart, the housemaster, 'fancied a great likeness between the Valley of the Wey and the Valley of the Usk'. Stewart taught writing and arithmetic and, at the old Charterhouse in London, had lectured in chemistry.

At the end of the Cricket Quarter and School Year of 1875 came the inevitable exodus of the senior boys, which made room available in other Out-Houses. This allowed Aubrey to move to Gownboys at the beginning of the Oration Quarter, which was how Carthusians referred to their winter term. He was denied the privilege of wearing the full garb of the old Charterhouse Gownboys, as this had been modified somewhat at the time of the transfer from London. The old Gownboy had worn black Eton jacket, waistcoat, white collar, black trousers, shoes called 'gowsers', gowns, and for those in the Upper School 'trenchers' or mortar-boards, whereas a Lower School Gownboy sometimes wore a blue flannel cap.

Aubrey's new housemaster was the Rev. H. J. Evans, M.A., who later became Honorary Chaplain to the school, and he was responsible for the welfare of between fifty and sixty boys. An ordinary school day began with an awakening bell at 6.45 a.m., and was followed by toilets in 'cocks' or long rooms, morning service in chapel, first school, headmaster's 'calling over', if it was a Wednesday or Thursday, breakfast, second school, dinner, third school, games, music lessons, squad drills, extra-curricular activities, tea, banco for the Under School (preparation of work for the next day), work in hall or study for the Upper School, prayers and lights-out at 9.20 p.m. for the younger boys, and later for the older. There were several variations on this theme depending on status, time of year and, to a certain extent, personal vocation.

Aubrey started in the Upper School, and then after sixteen months moved to Form Under IV B. In May of 1877 he was promoted to Form Under IV A, and then moved to the Remove the following September. Progress through the school was decided solely on academic ability, and Aubrey's was unspectacularly average. He did not excel particularly at lessons, and after that flurry of form-changing settled into a steady groove in Remove A, which for all we know may not have been dissimilar in its goings-on to the more famous later counterpart at Greyfriars. Whether C. A. S. was ever a member of a Famous Five is pure speculation. Or could he have provided the seed for the character of Herbert Vernon Smith? Smithy the Bounder, hard as nails, cocking a snook at authority, and smoking in his study. After all, it is known that 'Charles Hamilton followed the policy of ideas of such schools as Dulwich, Rugby and Charterhouse to teach boys to be good losers in the world of sport, businees and society, and to put up with petty trouble and inconveniences without sneaking and complaining.'

Aubrey's Remove form was a half-way stage through the school, and it was reached with a sense of achievement and relief, as it meant exemption from fagging for the majority. Fagging at Charterhouse, as in most public schools, entailed making breakfast and tea for Monitors, the cleaning of studies and being a general dogsbody. For a short time in his first year at the school, Aubrey had been fag to Robert Baden-Powell who, of course, was later to win fame as defender of Mafeking and founder of the Boy Scouts. At Charterhouse, Baden-Powell played in goal at football and used to practise a kind of one-upmanship of which Stephen Potter would have been proud. At half-time he would yell 'Boy', and demand a clean pair of boots, thereby giving the impression for the start of the second half that the opposition had been nowhere near his goal.

The power of the Monitors at Charterhouse was little less than absolute and behoved careful treading by lesser mortals. They were responsible for the discipline of the Under School, and kept a School Monitors book which listed instances of misdemeanour and the punishment exacted. The name C. A. Smith is to be found with some frequency – inattentive, absent from extra school, imposition not done, troublesome, disorderly, fighting. It would seem Aubrey was a spirited boy with a strong rebellious streak, and school photographs reveal the slightly sullen expression of somebody who is not quite at terms with himself or his surroundings. In these photographs he is often to be found posing awkwardly and independently at the end of a row, and obviously at times this period of teenage transition away from home comforts was difficult.

Aubrey stayed in the Remove for a year and two quarters, and he had to wait until May of 1879 to move upwards to Form Under V B. There was a further period of 'static growth' until the beginning of the Long Quarter in January of 1881, when he moved for the final six months of his school life to Form V, from where he was in a position to take the same university entrance exams as if he had been in the sixth form. The last two years at Charterhouse had been more fulfilling. He was a member of the School Fire Brigade, he had competed in the Pole Jump at the Athletic Sports of 1880 wearing a fetching chocolate and pink hooped jersey, and he had managed to get to the third round of the Double Lawn Tennis

Ties in the same year with his partner, Erskine minor. He also played football for his house, and in a game between Gown-boys and Girdlestoneites we read that 'Escombe, by another magnificent kick, placed the ball just in front of the Girdlestone-ite goal through which it was forced by Smith.' Unfortunately it had not been enough to save his side from a 5-2 defeat.

More importantly though, Aubrey was now playing cricket for the Charterhouse First Eleven. He had benefited from the coaching of the old Surrey player Julius Caesar, who was landlord of the local 'Railway Inn' at Godalming. In 'dry' hours, if there was such a thing for poor Caesar who had an alcohol problem, the boys were taught how to keep a straight bat and bowl a crooked ball by Julius and his brother Fred, who also umpired the school matches.

Aubrey made his way into the team in 1880 playing for the Rest of the School against the Monitors, and achieved several excellent bowling performances against strong opposition. The fixture card was enterprising and varied; sides such as Vaga-bonds, Broadwater, Revellers, Exeter College, Oxford, Incog-niti and M.C.C., as well as school elevens from Westminster and Wellington. The two years that Aubrey was in the team were outstandingly successful ones for Charterhouse cricket; they were a strong all-round side and authorities at the time reckoned they were probably the best school eleven in England. In the M.C.C. match they managed 253 against the bowling of Midwinter, Rylott and Flowers, and in the match against Wellington College in June 1880, Charterhouse won by an innings and 43 runs, dismissing Wellington in their first innings for only 27, with C.A.S. taking 6 for 12 in 50 balls. He also performed well against Esher when the school side won easily. Aubrey took 5 for 18 out of a total of 56. He finished the season second in the bowling averages with 38 wickets for 439 runs. A summary of all the matches reveals that 'C.A. Smith bowled with great effect at the beginning of the season, but seemed to lose all sting. Poor field. Likely to improve as a bat.' A wry touch, that last remark. Aubrey had only scored 22 runs in 11 innings.

The following year Aubrey performed exceptionally well with the ball. He had match figures of 10 for 47 against Southern Division, took 3 for 69 against M.C.C., and then 6 for

36 versus Old Carthusians, a match the school won by an innings and 5 runs. The game against Westminster School played at Vincent Square was remarkable for the margin of victory. Charterhouse won by an innings and 177 runs. The chief destroyer was T. W. Blenkiron with match figures of 10 for 37, but Aubrey helped with 4 for 38. He also partnered Blenkiron in a substantial ninth wicket stand of which he scored 35. He topped the bowling averages for the year with 64 wickets at 9.11. The summary of the season reflects his worth without overstatement: 'A greatly improved bat and field. A very steady fast bowler, always on the wicket, and at times very difficult to play.'

There was a further match that Aubrey played in for Charterhouse after the School Year had finished. This took place at the Hove Ground, Brighton on the first two days of the holiday, and was against Gentlemen of Sussex. It resulted in a creditable draw, with Charterhouse scoring 192 and 262, and their opponents 210 and 59 for 0. C. W. Wright, who with Aubrey was to gain a 'blue' at Cambridge the following year, made 106 in the second innings for the school. The school magazine notes that 'it is the first match of the sort that the school has played since its removal from London – and a very pleasant innovation it proved for all connected with it. We must not forget to thank Mr Smith who so kindly arranged the match for us, for two very pleasant days at Brighton, and for the great hospitality which he showed to us.' Possibly the Mr Smith referred to was Aubrey's father and it had been forgotten that he was a doctor. The school library at Charterhouse contains several scrapbooks compiled by the Headmaster's wife, the kindly Mrs Haig Brown, who took a maternal interest in the doings of all Carthusians. In one of them there is an envelope containing pressed flowers, and it is inscribed: 'August 3rd and 4th – Brighton Cricket – from Mr and Mrs Smith'. Could it have been a pleasant way of saying farewell with thanks for Aubrey's formative years?

2/ Cambridge and Sussex

Aubrey's bowling performance at Charterhouse and also for several sides in the Brighton area attracted the attention of several of the Sussex C.C.C. committee. The local press had reported that a consensus of knowing judges (whoever they were) had no doubts that Aubrey was the best school bowler of the year, and this opinion was emphasised when for Cuckfield he took 7 for 15 against Ardingly College, and for Sheffield Park 8 wickets for an average of little over 2. The County team were having a very lean time, and the president of the club, Lord Sheffield, was concerned enough to pay for the coaching of young and promising players by two professionals, Alfred Shaw and William Mycroft. Mycroft had remembered Aubrey's bowling from his visit to Charterhouse with an M.C.C. side, and recommended his lordship to include the youngster in his Sheffield Eleven, who were to play Fifteen of Sussex. It was an unusual honour for one so young, and even though he had little chance to shine in the match from now on his progress would be watched with great interest. Would he make the eleven at Cambridge? And, if so, how would he fare against the County sides?

Aubrey entered St John's College, Cambridge on the 13th of October 1881 as a pensioner, which meant in effect that Uncle Fred was footing the bill. He was to read chemistry and physics with a view to following his father's career as a physician, though naturally enough his sporting interests, and a burgeoning awareness of acting as an agreeable pastime, made considerable inroads into the hours he spent with his studies. That December he received a note from a C. Carthew-Yorstoun, honorary secretary to the College Dramatic Group:

Dear Sir,

　I have the pleasure to inform you that last night at General Meeting of the 'Thespids' you were elected a member. Hoping to hear from you that you will join.

It is strange that Aubrey apparently had not shown any interest in acting while at Charterhouse, if we discount a press-ganged appearance as one of the forty thieves in a production of *Ali Baba*. There were plenty of opportunities: the Headmaster, Haig Brown, frequently invited professional and amateur groups to perform at the school, and also encouraged active participation in the many house productions and Saturday entertainments. Old Boys who had made a name in the theatre enjoyed returning to parade their accomplishments, with the prospect of a splendid repast with some of the staff and seniors after the performance, before taking a gig to the station to catch the last train back to town. The Thespian tradition at Charterhouse was strong: Henry Siddons, G. F. Kean, Sir Johnston Forbes Robertson, Cyril Maude – a contemporary of Aubrey's, who remembered him being called C. A. at school, and with whom he had played 'tip and run'. In later years, after Aubrey had left, actors still emerged with regularity, led by the irrepressible Ben Travers, and followed by Richard Murdoch, Richard Goolden, and more recently Nicky Henson.

　At Cambridge, though, for the first time in his life, Aubrey felt unrestricted and in some control of his destiny, and the chance to act presented itself as a rewarding means of self-expression. His first appearance with the Thespids was in the following February in an original domestic drama by Tom Taylor called *Payable on Demand*. Aubrey took the leading rôle of Reuben Goldsched, a bankrupt Jew whose dubious scruples were no handicap on his way to becoming a prosperous merchant at the expense of a French Marquis. What human failings Aubrey had displayed to be considered for this rôle do not bear contemplation! Very possibly he was the only one enthusiastic, courageous or foolhardy enough to take on the part.

　Some time later, a repeat performance with an altered cast was mounted in the largest lecture room in St John's in aid of the Lady Margaret Boat Club. It went well in spite of there being only a couple of days' rehearsal. The College Chronicle records that 'C. A. Smith as Junius Brutus, a soldier of the French Republic, short though the character was, showed us that he is by no means a tiro in the Dramatic Art; he also 'under-read' S. T. Winkley's part (Reuben Goldsched), and gave it very well at the dress-rehearsal.'

In the Lent term of 1881, Aubrey was elected to the Eagles and became a fully fledged member of the sporting fraternity at St John's. He was also elected to the Inexpressibles, an exclusive club consisting of not more than sixteen resident members of the College. They liked to contest anything worth contesting with other clubs of similar exclusivity such as the Hawks. A fellow Inexpressible during Aubrey's third year with the club was Humphrey Rolleston, later physican to King George V.

The arrival of summer brought cricket's inescapable and welcome call, and Aubrey was not slow in responding. The twelve a side Freshman's Match was played over the first two days in May. Aubrey managed to take 8 for 60, and was immediately selected for the Next Sixteen against the First Twelve two days later. Again he played well. Twenty-one with the bat, and nine wickets for only thirty runs. He was now in the Cambridge side for the match against the M.C.C. and Ground to be played the following week.

The game was again twelve a side, and the Metropolitan team arrived with a strong bowling line-up, which included Flowers, Mycroft and Midwinter, who found a singular niche in cricket's *bizarrerie* column as the only man to play for both Australia and England. Their batting, though, was decidedly weak, and Aubrey took full advantage in the second innings when he routed the opposition with 5 for 17 off 20.3 overs of which 14 were maidens. *Wisden* noted that 'the bowling of Messrs Ramsay and Smith was so exceedingly good, that the first five wickets fell for 14 runs.' M.C.C. and Ground were all out for 46, and Cambridge had won by 189 runs.

The next match was against C. I. Thornton's XI, or an Eleven of England as it is sometimes called. W. J. Ford's *History of the Cambridge University Cricket Club* reports that 'the Cambridge eleven cut up very badly in this match, none of the batsmen doing anything except J. E. K. Studd, and Maynard ... and of the bowlers, only Roe who went on quite late meeting with any success ... the other bowlers were cut to ribbons.' Purely statistically, this would seem an inaccurate and unfair assessment, as C. T. Studd bowled 93.1 overs to take 3 wickets for 82 runs, and Aubrey bowled 45 overs and took 2 for 78. Roe acquired 3 for 17 off 13. Even allowing for four-ball overs, it is far from the annihilation the report suggests, and at least the bowlers deserved an accolade for stamina. Thornton's XI scored 384, with A. P. Lucas, G. F. Vernon, and S. S. Schultz making most of the runs, and the University lost the match by an innings and 92. It was during this match that Aubrey earned the sobriquet that was to stay with him throughout his life. When at Charterhouse, he had had trouble preventing himself from bowling far too much down the leg side, so he had devised a corrective plan whereby he approached from an angle and bowled round the wicket: 'C. I. Thornton was at the wickets, and I was ready to begin the bowling standing, as usual, somewhere near mid-off. Thornton stood at ease waiting for me to get into the proper place from which to bowl; on my part I was waiting for him to put himself into position. At last he said: "Why, you are not coming round the corner, are you?" Of course, I was christened "Round the Corner" on the spot.'

The original 'Round the Corner' Smith was a Hampshire gentleman who was inflicted with a troublesome speech impediment in R. S. Surtees' *Handley Cross or Mr Jorrocks's Hunt*, which had first been published in 1854. He was supposed to be in his late thirties, and was a natty dresser, fond of colourful double-breasted shawl waistcoats hung with Venetian chains; he patronised the waters at Handley Cross Spa and lodged round the corner of Hookem's Library, hence Round the Corner Smith. Nothing like Aubrey at all, whose splendid physique and fair hair made him look like a young Viking, but it was too good a nickname not to stick.

Aubrey's run up to the wicket caused comment throughout his cricketing career, and long after it was over. 'After a long run up, he came with a wide sweep from far on the other side, having the effect of concealing his approach and delivery never since emulated,' is the account we get from Sir Home Gordon, Bt. 'Sometimes he started from a deep mid-off position, at others from behind the umpire, and as described by W. G. Grace, "It is rather startling when he appears at the bowling crease," ' is Hubert Preston's summary. 'He was a slow bowler – slow to the point of slow motion who used to start his run about mid-off and then, as though by an after-thought, bowled round the wicket,' is the gospel according to A. A. Thomson. Others describe 'his oblique approach when bowling his off-breaks', or say, 'he was a slow bowler who, after marking out a straight run-up to the wicket, took a few steps towards mid-off,' so in order to add to the confusion let us return to Crusoe who was assured by an eminent player-critic (unnamed) that, when bowling, 'Smith did not arrive from round any corner at all, but approached on a logarithmic curve, and bowled as if the wind was always behind him.'

Obviously there is a lot of common ground in all these descriptions, and it is fairly clear that Aubrey had several variations in his approach, even if he had yet to resort to running backwards to the wicket and bowling over his head. What is not pointed out is that during his time with Charterhouse, Cambridge, Sussex and England, he often opened the bowling at a brisk fast-medium (rather like John Price of Middlesex) or was first change: 'tall and strong he had a high action and persistent accuracy, cutting the ball in from the off with purpose rather than subtlety,' and was often referred to as the best amateur fast bowler in the country.

Aubrey was now enjoying a period of intense activity at Cambridge. Immediately after the match against Thornton's XI came his initiation against a full county side, Lancashire, one of the two most powerful County combinations at that time. He had been chosen also to make his debut for Sussex against Derbyshire at Brighton at the beginning of June, and as if that were not enough, his evenings were being spent busily rehearsing the part of Henri de Flavigneul in the Thespids production of *The Ladies Battle*, which was to be his first romantic leading rôle. It was really rather tough on him as the rôle required extremely imaginative acting, for the part of the Countess d'Autreval, which was the feminine lead, was being played in 'drag' by one W. Sutherland-Stayner, who sounds as if he might have had a decidedly Calvinistic 'bent'. With all this activity, it is not hard to estimate the amount of time Aubrey was able to give to physics and chemistry.

The Lancashire match was a triumph for Cambridge. An

exciting and low scoring game in which C. T. and G. B. Studd made major batting contributions, ended with a narrow win for the Varsity by fourteen runs. Aubrey did not make any great impact, though his single scalp in each innings could not have been more valuable. 'Oh my Hornby and my Barlow of long ago.' Barlow was to get his revenge a month later in the return fixture at Old Trafford, when he bowled Aubrey for a duck.

His debut for Sussex was sound rather than spectacular. Sixteen in the first innings before being dismissed by his canny and friendly adversary of several contests, Mycroft, who by this time probably had a good idea of the best way to get Aubrey out, and fifteen in the second. In Derbyshire's first innings, Aubrey bowled 22 overs for 59 runs, and in their second, 10 overs for 11 runs and 1 wicket.

In the next few weeks Aubrey must have become thoroughly sick of the sight of Surrey. He played against them three times, once for Cambridge and twice for Sussex. The University's defeat broke a run of eight victories – Aubrey took 3 for 18 in Surrey's first innings, bowled only seven overs in their second, and his side were comprehensively beaten by seven wickets. In the second match for Sussex at the Oval, the situation was very different. 'For the first time since 1876 Sussex defeated Surrey, their victory on this occasion being in great measure due to the excellent bowling of Mr C. A. Smith of the Cambridge University eleven who took 8 wickets for 73 runs,' writes *Wisden*. His victims included fellow old Carthusian, E. O. Powell, who was captain of the eleven in 1879, the year before Aubrey found his way into the side.

The season for Cambridge finished with two matches at Lord's. In the game against M.C.C. we are told that 'Mr Smith joined Mr Ramsay in the first innings of Cambridge. Mr Smith played carefully and correctly, and Mr Ramsay hit brilliantly and the two put on 78 runs for the last wicket.' Mr Ramsay and Mr Smith also took the bulk of the wickets, 9 and 7 respectively. Even though the M.C.C. side was strong, and A. N. Hornby made a fifty and an undefeated century, Cambridge emerged easy winners by 163 runs.

Cambridge approached the Varsity Match confidently, in the knowledge that they had had a good year. They were a powerful combination captained by George Studd, who was a dashing batsman, fine ground fielder, and sometimes faulty catcher due to tiny hands that a facetious observer might think occasionally froze. He and his brother J.E.K. opened the batting, and were followed in turn by the Honourable M.B. Hawke, the very same Lord Hawke who, as the martinet captain of Yorkshire, ordered or was it sympathetically led Bobby Peel back to the pavilion for peeing on the pitch; F.E. Lacey, who once made 323 for Hants against Norfolk, and later was to be Secretary to the M.C.C.; another Studd brother, Charles, one of the great classically correct batsmen of his day, and a monotonously accurate slow bowler who was to become a missionary (incidentally, two of the Studds went into the church, and the other became Lord Mayor of London); C.W. Wright, 'Chawles', another old Carthusian who was an able wicket-keeper who played also for Notts; P.J.T. Henery and P.J. de Paravicini, both amateurs for Middlesex; R.C. Ramsay, 'Twisting Tommy', who was occasionally unplayable with his leg breaks; F.D. Gaddum; and Aubrey. The side had won five of their nine matches, and drawn two; they had achieved an outstanding win against the Australian tourists, and even though the startling defeat against Oxford the previous year was still fresh in the minds of some, this year there was no reason to doubt their ability to play to their full potential.

In the event the confidence was fully justified as Cambridge won by seven wickets, and it is a curious fact that for the next four years seven wickets was to be the margin between the two elevens. In 1882, the match was won by the Studds. George made a scintillating 120 in Cambridge's first innings, and Charles took 7 for 54 in Oxford's. Then in the Oxford second innings George engineered two extraordinarily adept pieces of run-out from mid-off. Aubrey bowled 57 overs in the match, 25 of them being maidens, and took 3 wickets for 68 runs, so he provided steady support. He made 14 batting at number ten.

In college matches for St John's during the summer Aubrey had scored 222 runs from 7 innings with a highest score of 60, and taken 21 wickets for 303 runs from 738 balls.

Aubrey's batting, which improved immeasurably after he left Cambridge in 1885, was positive and aggressive. Adjectives such as adventurous and hard-hitting abound in the reportage of his innings. Another old Carthusian, the writer R.C.

Robertson-Glasgow, 'Crusoe' to all who knew him and some who did not, conjures an immediate mental picture of Aubrey's batting. 'He was a long-reaching batsman of both vigilance and power, restrained from riotous hitting only by respect for convention.'

In Sussex's match against Kent at Brighton just after the University term had finished in July of 1882, it was described slightly differently although the image remains unchanged. 'Sussex, who batted first, lost 8 of their best wickets for 70 runs. Then, however, Mr Smith and H. Phillips got together and completely altered the aspect of the game. The Kentish bowling was severely punished and it was not until 95 runs had been added that Mr Smith was caught for a somewhat lucky innings of 68.' Then again, in August of that year in the fixture against Hampshire at Portsmouth: 'Mr Whitfield and Mr Smith played sterling cricket for their scores of 58 and 51 respectively, the former's innings being characterised by great care and precision, while the latter batted merrily ... Mr Smith made 51 out of 78 and his chief hits were six 4's and seven 3's.'

Ten days earlier, also at Portsmouth, C. A. S. had helped Cambridge University Past and Present to inflict the third defeat of their tour on the Australians. His bowling analysis for the first innings reads: 11.1 overs, 5 maidens, 16 runs, 4 wickets. The victims were Bannerman, Horan, Boyle and Spofforth.

On his return to University Aubrey had a great deal of catching up to do in regard to reading and practice of physics and chemistry. Inevitably his studies had suffered from the surfeit of cricket, and his involvement with the Thespids had not helped either. The sporting urge refused to remain dormant, however, and before long he was playing football regularly for the College eleven. Breath-taking touchline forays at outside right still left him with enough energy to squander on *Still Waters Run Deep*, another of those three-act comedies by Tom Taylor that seemed so popular with the Thespids. Aubrey's total immersion in anything that interested him can be seen by the fact that no only was he taking a leading part in the production as Captain Hawksley, but was also vice-president and acting stage manager for the company. Both jobs must have entailed a great deal of time organising people and paraphernalia, but as so often happens in small societies, enthusiasm and responsibility became the same the same thing.

The Thespids next presented a double bill in March of 1883, and Aubrey had parts in both productions. In *Our Bitterest Foe* by G. C. Herbert, which was based on an incident in the Franco-Prussian War in 1870, he played Henri de la Frère, an officer in the French Army who was in heavy disguise, and the other two characters were Blanche d'Evran who was his cousin, played by W. Sutherland-Stayner, obviously a 'soft touch' in travesty, and General Von Rosenberg, a Prussian commander acted by F. L. Thompson. The second half of the bill was a dramatic sketch in water colour by J. W. Jones called *On An Island.* The setting was Henholm Island on Lake Windermere which was represented in the most uncluttered, effective and inexpensive way possible, by putting a large moth-eaten mat on the floor of the lecture room. The sketch was a simple two-hander between a barrister-at-law, Jack Carlyon, played by C. A. S. and Milly Garland of Curzon Street, Mayfair, played by the ubiquitous W. S-S. Without knowing what happened *On An Island,* it would be impertinent to suggest that Milly could have been one of the more dubious denizens of that particular area of London, though the programme quote from *Much Ado About Nothing* offers endless possibilities. 'Some Cupid kills with arrows: some with traps.'

The Thespids' following productions played to standing room only on two nights at the beginning of June. Aubrey had sensibly acknowledged the demands of the cricket season by giving up the vice-presidency and acting stage managership, and only allowed himself to be co-opted into the comparatively undemanding off-stage rôle of treasurer. On stage, though, he was as ambitious as ever. Again it was a double bill and he acted in both. Moncrieff's two-act farce *The Spectre Bridegroom* or *A Ghost in spite of himself,* which had first been performed at the Theatre Royal, Drury Lane, over sixty years earlier, saw Aubrey don a white wig for the part of the poor bemused Dickory who illustrates two of the traditional elements of the genre – that of mistaken identity and misapprehension.

> *Enter Dickory, crying L.*
> *Aldwinkle:* Well, what the devil is that cursed long face for?

Dickory: Oh master! – oh, Mr Aldwinkle, such a misfortune! Oh! Oh!

Aldwinkle: What! I suppose, when you got to the half-way house, you found Mr Nicodemus had just departed?

Dickory: Yes, poor gentleman, he'd been quite gone an hour afore I'd got there. I helped to lay him out, when I found how things were.

Aldwinkle: Lay him out. Zounds, I hope you didn't speak anything ill of him.

Dickory: Oh no, master, we never do speak ill of those who are gone.

Aldwinkle: Gone! – Well, but he's come.

Dickory: Come – what! – Ha'they brought his body here?

Aldwinkle: No, he brought his body here himself.

Dickory: What! – In a hearse?

Aldwinkle: No – on a horse – and you must go and wait on him.

Dickory: What! – Sit up all night wi' him?

Aldwinkle: No; only till he's finished his supper.

Dickory: His supper?

Aldwinkle: His supper – yes blockhead – his supper; he's just sat down with my daughter.

Dickory: Dang it, this be the first time I ever heard of dead men sitting down to supper wi' young ladies – he be quite mad; how his eyes do roll! Surely—

All highly unlikely, and of course the almost conditioned reflex of the cross-purpose conversation is half the fun of it for the audience. *Ibid* was complimentary: 'Mr C. A. Smith as Dickory gave us the best piece of acting during the evening. He may be said to have created the character, as he chose to represent Dickory as a very old man bent almost double, with a voice turning again towards childish treble. He alone seemed to have that command over the muscles of his face which is essential to real acting.'

The other farce on the programme was in one act, and was set in Corsica. *A Thumping Legacy* by J. Maddison Morton contained characters whose names gave but the merest hint of their disposition. We need go no further than 'Jerry Ominous'. The character that Aubrey played sounds full of villainy and decidedly Cosa Nostra. Bambogetti, even if not an Italian waiter, was bound to have had a finger in more than one pie.

Aubrey had made several excursions on to the cricket field during the rehearsal period for these farces and, in the trial match at the beginning of the season, as a resident 'blue', he had naturally been chosen to represent the First Twelve against the Next Sixteen. *Wisden's Almanack* covering the events of last season had just been issued. Some sentences in the summary of Sussex cricket must have rankled. After laudatory comments on the bowling potential of A. Hide, J. Seneschal and W. Tester, it was asserted that the 'bowling of Lillywhite, W. Humphreys, Mr Blackman and Mr C. A. Smith, all of whom had a good deal of work with the ball, proved expensive.' Although there was consolation in being part of distinguished company, justice could have been served by pointing out that he was an inexperienced nineteen-year-old finding his way in a most testing arena without much support. Admittedly, his 14 wickets in seven first class matches for Sussex had cost 339 runs from 177 overs, but at no time had he been collared, and against Surrey his bowling had been decisive. A sufficient spur no doubt to send him into the match against the Freshmen determined to do well. He did so, taking 7 for 50, and then, in the first innings of the following match against the M.C.C., 3 for 38 off 28 overs, 17 of which were maidens. Rain spoilt the match, a new pitch had to be cut on the second day, batting was at a premium, and Cambridge were routed by the bowling of Rylott and Flowers.

After turning out for Sussex against Hampshire at Brighton where he would have seemed to have justified his place by taking 4 for 26 in the second innings, Aubrey was not included in the Cambridge eleven for the next two matches against C. I. Thornton's XI and Yorkshire. He was dropped for slackness in the field, a fact that many would find difficult to believe in the years to come. However, he was reinstated for the game against the Gentlemen of England which Cambridge won by eight wickets, thanks mainly to the two Charles's, Wright and Studd, who both scored 71 not out in their second innings.

With the distraction of the Thespids out of the way until autumn, Aubrey was able to concentrate more on cricket, and he immediately took advantage of this in the game against the Orleans Club at Twickenham. After J. E. K. Studd, the Hon.

J. W. Mansfield and P. J. T. Henery had made substantial batting contributions in the Cambridge total of 381, Aubrey bowled the side to a comfortable victory by taking 6 for 62 in the last innings.

The Cambridge eleven stayed in London overnight, and began a match against Surrey at the Oval the next day. The game was memorable for a superb second innings of 115 not out by C. T. Studd over three and three-quarter hours. Cambridge totalled 307 and won by 200 runs. Aubrey had bowled extremely accurately in the Surrey first innings, acquiring 4 for 44 off 35.1 overs.

The only side to beat Cambridge that year had been the M.C.C. in the opening game, so the return fixture promised to be hotly contested. P. J. de Paravicini top scored for 40 in Cambridge's first knock, and C. A. S., batting at number ten, hit 31, which was the second highest score. The same pair took the bowling honours with three wickets apiece for relatively little and the M.C.C. deficit on the first innings was 51. Cambridge then extended their lead to 294 with J. E. K. Studd and de Paravicini each hitting 60s and eventually the M.C.C. fell short by 81 runs.

The M.C.C. match always provided an ideal preparation for the encounter that really mattered. The Freshmen particularly found that playing at Lord's one week before the game against Oxford helped them get used to the big match atmosphere and made the Varsity match just a little less of an ordeal, though that does not imply that muscles were any less taut when the large, fashionably-dressed crowd came into view on the long walk to the crease.

Cambridge batted first and made 215, largely due to C. W. Wright, who patiently accumulated 102. Disaster then hit Oxford in the shape of C. T. Studd and C. A. Smith. They were all out for 55 with Studd taking four wickets and Aubrey three on a pitch that was giving the bowlers help, but not as much as might have been assumed. Aubrey had also snatched three catches, which is a reminder of Robertson-Glasgow's line, 'that at slip he excelled, having enormous hands and the telescopic arm.'

Having followed on, Oxford fared better, but not well enough. They emulated the Cambridge first innings total of

215 with Studd again capturing 4 wickets, but this time C. A. S. outdid him by taking 6 for 78 off 58 overs, 24 of which were maidens. The feat was even more noteworthy for the fact that the six wickets had come from the first seven in the Oxford batting order, and then to add further damage Aubrey had caught the last man, Bastard, off the bowling of Studd to bring the Oxford innings to a close. Hard as Hine-Haycock, Grant-Asher, Ruggles-Brise *et al* had fought, there were but 56 runs for Cambridge to make, and this they achieved for the loss of three wickets.

The Cambridge University Cricket Club had the match ball mounted and presented to Aubrey in honour of his outstanding contribution to the victory, 9 for 106 from 80 overs, four catches, two run-outs, and therefore a hand in fifteen of the twenty dismissals.

During his six matches for the Varsity he had managed to take 29 wickets for 490 runs, and in college matches for St John's he had come out top both in the batting and bowling averages by scoring 241 runs from 6 innings with a highest score of 118 for an average of 48.1, and taking 26 wickets from 614 balls for 10.4.

Aubrey's 1883 cricket season ended with three games for Sussex, and afternoons with local club sides. Two of the county games were against Surrey, and in the first at the Oval he took 5 for 89 off 40.2 overs, though in the return at Brighton he had to be content with the wicket of Abel. The diminutive and talented Abel was in danger of becoming a C. A. S. 'rabbit' as it was the third time that Aubrey had 'bagged' him during the season.

Back at St John's, with the 'stinks' of the chemistry lab providing a pungent reminder that this was exam year, Aubrey did not allow this alarming thought to interfere with his election as captain of the college football team. Nor did the essential examination of H_2SO_4 and its more advanced cousins in any way preclude the dedicated enjoyment of rehearsing for the Thespids' winter production of *Weak Woman*. Aubrey was now installed as president of the company, on condition that he did not allow ladies to participate in productions, and was therefore relieved of the sordid business of chasing subs from dilatory members. As usual, the Thespids presented two pieces, although the new president did make more than a token gesture to his other commitments by appearing in only one of them. So, on the evening of December 7th, Lecture Room 4 was the place to be.

On stage first was Maddison Morton's *John Dobbs*, which when reviewed in the *College Chronicle* drew only muted praise. The magazine then tells its readers that 'the farce was followed by *Weak Woman*, a three-act comedy from the prolific pen of the late H. J. Byron, and is of that class of comedy which he knew so well how to construct. Though inferior in plot to many of his plays, it shows that daring conception of comic character and that marvellous aptitude of bright repartee which will make the loss of poor Harry Byron a difficult one to replace. In our opinion the farcical love scene at the end of the third act, where Ginger proposes to Mrs Gunn (under the false impression that she has come in to money) and finds her fair form far too heavy for his manly knees, is among the most absurd that the author has ever conceived, and, as played by the Thespids, it convulsed the house.'

Our Chronicle goes on to dissect the performance of the cast, and we find that 'Mr C. A. Smith – on whose shoulders rested the serious interest of the piece – played Fred Fanshawe in a thoroughly competent manner, and, despite his mannerisms, fully deserves his reputation as the leading actor of the Club. Mr Smith has an exceptionally fine stage presence, which on a larger stage would be an even greater advantage, but why will he try to spoil it by stooping? If he would only overcome this fault he has every requisite for a successful lover.' Aubrey must have been delighted with this last comment!

Aubrey's theatrical leanings and ambitions had naturally attracted wider attention than from the college inmates of St John's, and since he was also a member of the Cambridge Amateur Dramatic Company and had helped with their production of *The Goose With the Golden Eggs* the previous February, it is not surprising to find him taking the role of De Neuville, who was secretary to the legitimist Marquis de Cevennes, in the drama *Plot and Passion* which was set in the Paris and Prague of 1810. The part gave him an opportunity to exercise his technique in scenes of amorous dalliance with Mr J. R. Manners, who played Madame de Fontanges.

His next outing with the A.D.C. in March of 1884 was set in far less sophisticated surroundings as Farmer Wheatear in *My Turn Next*. Then came the part of Tom Conyers in F. W. Broughton's comedietta *Withered Leaves* in June of the same year, and *Our Chronicle* felt obliged to remind any who had somehow forgotten that 'in the late A.D.C. performances C. A. Smith, Howarth and G. F. G. Dill all took prominent parts in the plays, and of the four actors especially picked out and most favourably criticised we are proud to state that three were either present or past Thespids.'

The University cricket season had started towards the end of May with the annual fixture against C. I. Thornton's XI. The captain for the summer was J. E. K. Studd, which neatly rounded off the Studd dynasty at Cambridge, as his brothers George and Charles had been in charge of the eleven successively in the two previous years. J. E. K. had a lot to live up to, as those two years had been highly successful ones for the team. This season though turned out differently, as is seen in W. J. Ford's précis of the game at Fenners versus Thornton's: 'As was the case in most of the matches of this year of disaster, the best cricket of the match was shown by the opponents of Cambridge ... not that Studd and Paravicini did not bat well or Smith bowl successfully, but the side failed as a side, and lost the match by 113 runs.' Aubrey's consolation was 4 for 36 and 3 for 48.

The sole victory of the Cambridge season came in the next game that Aubrey played in against a strong 'Gentlemen of England' side, though the margin was the narrow one of twelve runs. The Australians came in the middle of June, and exacted considerable revenge for their defeat two seasons earlier, in winning by an innings and 81 runs – the first time they had beaten the University. Aubrey obtained George Giffen's wicket while conceding 83 runs in 54 overs.

The next game was against Surrey at the Oval where Aubrey managed to take 5 for 88 off 46 overs in the first innings. Cambridge lost by 148 runs.

The twelve a side game against the M.C.C. will always be known as Flowers' match. He not only scored 122 out of 157, hitting eighteen fours, but captured fourteen of the twenty-two wickets at a cost of less than six runs each. The result was another innings defeat for the University, and apart from taking 3 for 50 Aubrey distinguished himself by being dismissed for a 'pair' by the flushed Flowers.

And so to Lord's and the University match, with the sides' records exactly reversed. Oxford had won six games and lost one, and Cambridge had won one and lost six, so there was no doubt who were favourites. The game itself was a lifeless affair and consequently disappointing; there was no piece of outstanding cricket to give it 'spark', and therefore the match unfolded along a predictable pattern towards what was now the pre-ordained victory margin of seven wickets. Only this time, of course, it was for Oxford. Aubrey manufactured three doubles in the match, two catches, two wickets, those of Brain and Bastard, and again two noughts, not out in each case.

A post-mortem report on the failures of the season states that 'it is no secret that the side was not a homogeneous one – nor did they pull well together.' Such is the difference that can be caused by four new faces. Aubrey had played in six of the matches, and taken twenty wickets at a cost of 531 runs. For St John's he had batted four times, and scored 107 runs, and bowled 298 balls and acquired fifteen wickets.

Aubrey did not play for Sussex in 1884, who were having their best season for some time, though he did turn out for the Gentlemen of Sussex against the Gentlemen of Philadelphia, whose tour had suffered somewhat in the shade of the visiting Australians.

The *Brighton Herald* reported that the home side were comprised of the 'finest Sussex amateurs that could be placed in the field' and that 'Mr R. K. Sampson, Mr A. Blackman, Mr W. Blackman, Mr R. T. Ellis, Mr G. Brown and Mr C. A. Smith were in excellent trim.' Aubrey hit freely for his 33, and took one wicket.

That June had been an exhaustingly busy month. He had been examined and approved in a First Examinations for an M.B. Degree in Chemistry and Physics; he had taken a Special Examination in Natural Sciences for the Ordinary B.A. Degree, with the resultant placing of Chemistry Class II; he had spent at least twelve days playing cricket, and given over a number of evenings to rehearse and finally perform in *Withered Leaves*, and assist with *Helping Hands*. At the end of that period no doubt he felt like one, and could have done with the other!

The University Calendar for 1884 records that the persons whose B.A.'s fall into the Class II category will complete them on the 19th December, and sure enough in the listing for January of 1885 is found C. A. Smith, *Artium Baccalaurei Ordinarii Classis 2da.*

That winter he again appeared for the A.D.C. as Tom Dexter in *The Overland Route* and Faturs in *The Census,* and he was still captaining the St John's Association Football Club, which was the rather grandiose way in which they liked to be known.

A volume of the *Eagle Chronicle* compares this year's side rather unfavourably with that of last, and gives their view on why there were only as they call it 'meagre results'. 'The fault that chiefly struck us in the team was the want of combination which we think was greatly owing to the fact that we had no efficient centres, our captain, who is chiefly distinguished for his play on the right, having at times to sacrifice himself to the exigencies of the occasion, and play in the centre ... C. A. Smith captained the team well throughout, having more than usual difficulties to contend with.' The club won three of their games, drew four, and lost five.

In February a morning performance of the comedy *Old Soldiers* was mounted at the Theatre Royal, Brighton, with the proceeds going towards the purchase of the Sussex County Cricket Ground. Aubrey helped with the staging, and also took the part of the young country gent, Lionel Leveret.

When it came to the cricket season at Cambridge the trial fixture between the Freshmen and the Eleven was drawn after an interesting tussle that left the seniors with 47 to get and six wickets in hand. Aubrey was in fine fettle, getting seven wickets in the second innings and making 71 not out in very quick time. He only played in four matches for the University that year, as throughout May and early June he was appearing for Sussex. He therefore missed the fixture against 'Buns' Thornton's XI, where three wickets had fallen before it was discovered that the pitch was a yard and a half too long, and the game had to be restarted.

Sussex had a very poor season. They had lost several

stalwarts from the previous year, which had been comparatively very successful, and this left their bowling the weakest of the nine leading counties. The batting was not much better. Their supporters' disappointment found some outlet in vituperative letters to the local press. A few of the correspondents thought Aubrey was not worth his place in the side, and was only included because he was an amateur; if one considers figures alone, perhaps they had a point, though apart from Juniper he bowled as well as any and always very economically.

The sight of his old stamping ground at Fenners in June, however, seemed to give Aubrey just the spur he needed. Here he was playing for his county side, Sussex, against his University who were led by the Hon. M. R. Hawke. It must have felt strange turning out against his old team mates, and he was to take advantage of his knowledge of their batting limitations in a spectacular way. The pitch was rain-affected, and Juniper exploited this to the tune of 7 for 24 as Cambridge plummeted to 86 all out. Sussex fared even more disastrously; their innings which had begun at 3.15 ended at five past five. 75 all out, and C. A. S. coming in at number eight had carried his bat for three. The day ended with Cambridge 51 for 2.

Wisden's Almanack records that 'the game was resumed at 11.30 on the Wednesday and the remaining 8 wickets fell for an addition of 68 to the overnight total, the fast bowling of Mr Smith meeting with extraordinary success.' In eighteen overs of which thirteen were maidens, Aubrey swept aside Cambridge with five wickets for only eight runs, clean bowling four, and Sussex spent the afternoon gathering the runs they needed to win by seven wickets.

By one of these strange quirks of fate, it is quite likely that Aubrey would not have had the chance to shoulder the responsibility of the bowling on the last day if Juniper, who had bowled so well in the first innings, had not become unwell. In fact, poor Juniper bowled his last overs for Sussex that morning, as he had contracted an illness which ultimately led to his death. Such are the wheels of chance and mischance, for without that devastating spell Aubrey would not have been selected to join the University XI for the remainder of their season. 'I was lucky in getting my "blue" in the fourth year as I had gone down.' Prior to the encounter with Oxford there were games against Yorkshire, Surrey and M.C.C., but eventually the climax to the Varsity season arrived.

'Before the match I was offered 100 to 1 about the exact result. I said seven wickets.' It had to be, and as Aubrey felt that it was Cambridge's turn to win by that amount, it was necessary for Oxford to bat first. Toppin lived up to his name and took 7 for 54 as Oxford struggled for 136. Cambridge then passed that total without losing a wicket, until the innings fell away rather, and it was left to the splendid (tautological!) Toppin and C. A. S., batting at numbers ten and eleven, to lift the total to 287. Aubrey's contribution had been a lively 23.

Oxford then fought a long rearguard action, and Aubrey sustained an accurate and hostile spell of bowling over 32 overs to hit the wicket five times for 57 runs, which included the dismissals of A. E. Newton and A. H. J. Cochrane in successive balls; Oxford had totalled 239 and Cambridge needed 89 to win. This they managed fairly easily, and in order to keep the four-year sequence intact, they lost three wickets in doing so. Aubrey's four matches for the side had produced 12 wickets for 362 runs at an average of just over 30, which was more expensive than his norm.

During the season he had taken the same amount of wickets in six matches for Sussex. There his average was improved by conceding only 280 runs.

The next few years were to be a time of trial and error for Aubrey; a transference from the relatively carefree and cultured cloisters of Cambridge to the more demanding and less esoteric world in which pounds, shillings and pence had to be earned for keep. Uncle Fred had paid so far, now it was up to Aubrey.

Looking back, he could feel that his time at University had been well spent. He had made a mark both at Cambridge and outside, and although he had no real pretensions towards the academic life, sporting prowess and to some extent public appearances in plays had given him a standing that was enviable.

'Standing' rarely pays bills, and Aubrey dispelled any inward doubts about his unspoken dislike of academia and accepted an offer from a friend at University to join him in teaching at an Army 'crammer' in Haywards Heath that was run by the friend's father. There, Aubrey taught Higher Mathematics to young cadets aspiring for Woolwich and Sandhurst, and no doubt explained in detail the complexities of Gunter's chain, and the diagonals of quadrilateral fields which had perpendiculars forced upon them from opposite angles, all of which formed part of the Militia Examination Papers at that time. Then, after the lessons were over, his pupils presumably found little respite when he acted as P.T. instructor and coerced the not so able and unwilling into a course of athletic exercise that lost nothing to militaristic charm. If money had been available at this stage Aubrey would have been tempted to pursue a full-time career as an officer in the Army, but it was not.

The 'cramming' establishment folded after a couple of years; it had not been well run and there were many other similar tutorials available at places such as 'Carlisle and Gregson' or 'Jimmy's' as it was known, which had the residential attraction of being situated in 'up-market' Kensington.

Working at Haywards Heath had given Aubrey the opportunity to continue his love affair with the stage. He appeared for the Brighton Green Room Club, and indeed lived in the town at 27 Selbourne Road, West Brighton. He was also continuing with football sporadically, turning out at outside right for Old Carthusians in the F.A. Cup. In March of 1885 he had played for them in a quarter-final against Church which they won 1-0, and again in the semi-final against Blackburn Rovers when they lost 1-5. Edward Grayson in his book *Corinthians and Cricketers* tells how a couple of years later Aubrey was at outside left in the Old Carthusian side which took on Preston North End in a quarter-final, virtually the last serious intrusion by an Old Boys' side into the F.A. Cup, after professionalism had been legalised in 1885. It was the season before the 'Invincibles' became the first to do the 'double' and Grayson quotes A. H. Tod, an assistant master at Charterhouse, as saying, 'Early in the game C. A. Smith had the professionals' goal at his mercy, when he was tripped from behind and the play then became decidedly rough.' O.C.'s, who had been one of the first sides to play the 'combination' game as inherited from Scotland, went down 2-1 after extra time, though Aubrey received a good deal of favourable comment on his several attempts to score.

He also played for the Old Boys against the school, and scored in the game in 1888, and appeared as well for Corinthians, who had a great forward line - Bambridge, Cobbold, Lindley, Braun, and either Spilsbury or Aubrey. Although he regarded football far less seriously than cricket, he could be relied upon to be in the thick of the action, even if his 'lankiness was a handicap for turning quickly.'

Aubrey's cricket in these bridging years was mostly confined to club sides, not all of whom were in the Brighton area, as appeared for Linton and also Bickley Park in Kent. On one occasion for Incogniti against Devonshire Park at Eastbourne he had figures that were practically Laker-like - with a hand in seventeen wickets out of the nineteen to fall to bowlers, the other being run out. In the first innings he clean-bowled seven, including the hat-trick, caught and bowled another and took two slip catches, thereby having a hand in all ten. In the second innings he clean-bowled six, and caught one at cover.

His teaching commitments in 1886 restricted his appearances for Sussex to three games in which he did little. The following season was to be very different.

'It has been decided that Mr C. A. Smith will replace Mr F. M. Lucas as Captain of Sussex for the season that will shortly be with us.'

In that matter-of-fact way did readers of the Brighton press learn that the amateur, who two years ago was thought not good enough to play for the County, was now to lead the effort to drag Sussex cricket away from the doldrums.

Lucas was to be unavailable for most of the season (before going to India and dying of cholera) and several influential voices on the committee had thought that Aubrey was the man for the job. They realised that he embodied the Carthusian traditions of leadership and versatility, was a man for the biggest of occasions and that he seemed to relish responsibility. They remembered his feat of 5 for 8 for the County when Juniper was taken ill.

Aubrey, uncharacteristically, had been at somewhat of a loose end; he had relinquished his teaching post, or rather there was no longer any post for him to relinquish, and he had long ago given up any thoughts of a medical career. While he enjoyed his acting interludes with the Green Room Club, it was not a full-time existence, and nor would a career on the stage have been thought suitable for a Varsity man. It was not until around the First World War that social attitudes mellowed towards 'rogues and vagabonds' coming from 'true blue' Universities and as the eminent critic W. A. Darlington has pointed out, Aubrey was one of the first to take that particular journey.

So, it was with a mixture of relief for something positive to do and concern about the impending difficulty of trying to extract the best from a dispirited side who had finished in the bottom two places in the County Championship for the last two years, that Aubrey accepted the captaincy.

Sussex started the season well. They beat M.C.C. and Ground at Lord's by four wickets, and C. A. S. took six wickets. This was the match during which the thirteen-year-old Pelham Warner went to Lord's for the first time, and thereafter remembered to his dying day seeing C. A. Smith dismiss F. E. Lacey. They then defeated Hampshire at Southampton by nine wickets with their new captain taking 3 for 24 from 22 overs in the first innings. A drawn game with Cambridge followed in glorious mid-June sunshine, with a light breeze from the sea to help dry sweat-sodden shirts; the pitch was perfect for batting, and nearly twelve hundred runs were scored during the three days while only twenty-five wickets went down.

Then came two matches against Kent, home and away. At Brighton, Sussex emerged triumphant winners by seven wickets with Aubrey clearly enjoying his captain's rôle in an innings of 43 not out. At Tonbridge, Kent came out on top by six wickets and *Wisden* suggested that 'perhaps the best thing of the first day was the bowling of Mr C. A. Smith who on the hard ground took 6 wickets for 52 runs, upsetting the middle stump four times.' The return fixture against Hampshire started on the following day at Brighton, and Sussex duly won by 185 runs. It was to be their last victory of the season.

A heavy defeat by Nottinghamshire started the tide towing the wrong way, and then a less emphatic loss to Gloucestershire in which C. A. S. grabbed a couple of twenties and a brace of Grace's, W. G. and E. M. The remaining encounters were drawn or lost narrowly with one exception, which was an even more massive defeat from the powerful Notts eleven in the return at Trent Bridge.

The only similarity in two remarkable games with Surrey had been Aubrey's achievement in taking nine wickets. On the last day of the match at Brighton, Surrey seemed to be heading for a comfortable victory when they had eight wickets to fall and 47 to get. C. A. S. and Arthur Hide obviously thought otherwise and in the end, amid scenes of rare excitement for Sussex supporters, Surrey only scraped home by one wicket. Aubrey had been 'in great form with the ball, and bowled with exceptional success' and it must have been a great disappointment to have had nothing to show for having come so close.

The final few hours of the away fixture at the Oval were played on a treacherous pitch which was the result of bad weather. There were extraordinary moments where the last Surrey batsmen were trying their hardest to get out quickly, and the Sussex bowlers were trying equally hard to prevent them doing so. Bowley of Surrey was running halfway up the pitch hoping he would be stumped, Dudney was refusing to take the bails off, and Bean was bowling eight no-balls in succession in order to prolong the innings and thereby save Sussex from having to bat too long on a tricky pitch. Eventually Bowley hit his own wicket, and Lohmann took all seven of the Sussex wickets to fall before the game was drawn.

What Aubrey thought about all this is difficult to imagine. Presumably as captain he sanctioned at least the Sussex side of the tactics, and possibly could have instigated them to offset the actions of Bowley. Maybe he was intrigued by the psychological intricacies of the situation, as he was a great one for theorising on radical measures the game could take. Nevertheless, such goings-on hardly constituted the spirit of cricket, and it would have been surprising if he approved, though as a relatively inexperienced captain he might not have thought of all the possible resultant ramifications at the time. Surely the body M.C.C. at Lord's would not have been pleased and could have been expected to issue a reproof.

Although Sussex had had a generally disappointing season, they had on many occasions played entertaining cricket. The morale of the side was better than before, and there was optimism for the future. *Wisden's* summary read: 'The bowling of the team was not formidable, but, considering the excellence of the Brighton wickets, Mr Smith and Arthur Hide did very well, Mr Smith indeed threw himself thoroughly into the county matches and was a most energetic, painstaking captain.' The rival *Lillywhite* complemented those remarks with 'On the hard wickets of last summer, the bowling did not seem to have much sting, and this notwithstanding that Mr C. A. Smith, who acted as captain – and a right good captain too – was generally successful.' These views were widespread. Aubrey's appointment was felt to have been a judicious move on the part of the committee: 'He had given good service personally, and had showed no small judgement in the management of his team.'

Aubrey had finished top of the Sussex bowling averages with 35 wickets at 20.12. He had also made an appearance for Gentlemen of Sussex in their nine-wicket victory against the Canadians, who were making an eight match tour, and had thoroughly demoralised their batsmen when taking eight wickets in their first innings. He had already shown his worth with the bat by making a stylish 44.

In minor matches, he had donned M.C.C. colours to devastate the Hurst College attack with 163 not out, and then found Mr Dill's Eleven even more to his liking when representing Burgess Hill, and made 168. For the same side he overwhelmed Cuckfield, and then Hurst with two nine-wicket hauls, conceding only two runs in the first instance, and seven in the second. In all games during the season, he went into bat forty-eight times for 1448 runs (av. 30.1), and persuaded the umpire to signal the dismissal of 198 batsmen for a tariff of 1750 runs (av. 8.8). Convincing support for the magazine *Cricket*, when it reasoned that 'Mr Smith may be fairly classed as one of the very best amateur bowlers of the day. On his form of 1887, in fact, it is open to question whether he has any superiors among amateurs as a fast bowler.'

3/Australia

The sun was scorching; some of the hottest temperatures on earth had been recorded a few miles away. The Orient liner S.S. *Iberia* had just left its latest port and last call, and was chugging unhurriedly into the Indian Ocean towards its destination. Many of the twenty-six cricketers on board were ill-prepared and unsuitably clad for the humidity of Aden, and were realising already that the chill draughts of approaching autumn back home had certain previously unappreciated attractions.

Australia would be hot as well, were the threatening promises given by more seasoned travellers and deckhands, who were busy reassembling the sporting para and diverting phernalia that was provided by the company for bored passengers in order to distract from their discomfort. And it was to be eight months, thought some of the cricketers, before they would return to Plymouth and put foot again on the reassuringly firm terra of England, and have the chance to greet leaden skies as a normal bestowal of nature rather than as an exception. As it turned out, the Australian summer was to be the wettest for many a year, but no one knew that then, of course, and so they looked forward to the evening when it would be a good deal cooler on board, with the prospect of finding light relief of another kind as they watched the Surrey pair Monty Bowden and W. W. Read join Aubrey and the rest of the aptly-named 'Thespiberians' in a performance of Byron's comedy *Old Soldiers*, that relied heavily on improvisation and much less on rehearsal.

The two teams of thirteen were embarking on what was described later as 'the most prominent case of folly in connection with cricket that has been undertaken to that date'. One side, managed by Mr G. F. Vernon and led by the Hon. M. R. Hawke, who became Lord Hawke when his father died during the course of the trip, necessitating his early return to England, had been invited to tour Australia by the Melbourne Club. The other team, assembled by Messrs Shaw, Shrewsbury and Lillywhite, and captained by Aubrey, had been asked to make the trip by the Sydney Association. The Melbourne authorities claimed that it had been widely known that their intention of bringing out an English side the year before had been merely postponed, whereas the Sydney group denied this and said that for all they knew the project had been abandoned. The ensuing wrangle between the rival parties was bitter and protracted, and inevitably the jealousies engendered cast a few shadows over the playing and social side of both tours.

Shrewsbury's team, as it was most often called, contained some formidable pros, players of the calibre of George Lohmann Maurice Read of Surrey, Johnny Briggs of Lancashire, and George Ulyett of Yorkshire, and these were backed up by three quality amateurs from Sussex, W. Newham, G. Brann and C. A. S., and one from Warwickshire, L.C. Docker.

The tour started near Sydney, with Shrewsbury's side getting much the better of a drawn game against eighteen lads from Parramatta. They had been greeted at the railway station by the mayor and representatives of the local clubs, and a dozen or so toasts were exchanged before everybody trooped, or rather tottered, down to the ground to try and justify their reason for being there. It was an all too predictable ritual with which the cricketers were to become inured as they travelled wearily from one sun-scalped outback town to another. The intentions of the welcoming troupes were of the best, which was not how the cricketers looked or felt, having often undergone a tortuous journey of up to eighteen hours in cramped and unsumptuous railway carriages. In those pre-air-conditioned days, suffocating heat had to be borne with fortitude, if not equanimity, and it was balm, if not Gilead, when occasionally the welcoming speeches were kept until after the team's arrival at an hotel and they had had a chance to recover a little from the rigours of the trek. When that happened, most home dignitaries spoke at length. Aubrey, replying, never did.

After the game against Parramatta, the team travelled back to Sydney for a few days most necessary net practice before taking on a strong New South Wales XI. There they found that getting attuned to the different bounce of Australian pitches was a more hazardous process than first imagined (the wicket was top-dressed with mud from the Harbour, and looked like slabs of Turkish Delight), and on a rain-affected strip several of the team captured a few knocks and bruises before being beaten convincingly by ten wickets. Having spent nearly two months at sea, it was obvious that most of the side had barely found their 'land legs', let alone any playing form, and their acclimatisation had not been assisted when a few days previously they had succumbed to the unavoidable dictates of official hospitality by taking a picnic trip in the Governor's launch down harbour.

All of the side, except Shrewsbury, had embarked on the excursion, although soon after leaving Prince's Stairs Aubrey, who had been feeling unwell all morning, began to wish that he had stayed at the hotel. He was suffering from 'a gathered ear', which was swollen with pus since being infected by an insect bite, and so as soon as the boat had reached Fort Macquarie he and George Lohmann, who nobly ignored Aubrey's pleas to stay on board and insisted on accompanying his skipper, were put ashore to make their own way back.

The infection had caused Aubrey to miss the game against N.S.W., albeit very reluctantly, and he spent a couple of days resting at the team quarters. He was well enough though to journey to Brisbane, and was determined to turn out in the next match. The game against Eighteen of Queensland was played at the new grounds of the National Association at Bowen Park, and on the first morning those with a financial stake in the tour must have felt a tremor or two when looking at the disappointingly sparse attendance of no more than a couple of hundred. Luckily for the promoters the Saturday afternoon sun attracted His Excellency the Governor, several members of Parliament and a few more less distinguished of the local populace, and so the headquarters band under Bandmaster Owen was able to add 'not a little to the enjoyment of the 5000 present'.

Aubrey opened the batting with George Brann and managed 'to hit several for a brace', as it was rather quaintly described in the *Brisbane Courier*, and when bowling 'got among the timbers with fast ones'. Nobody on either side made many runs, the bowlers on an unkempt pitch having it all their own way, and so the decision of the Star Ministrel Company, who were performing at the Gaiety Theatre, to present a silver cup to the highest scorers in the first innings seemed a trifle premature. The trophies were presented by Miss Nellie Langtry, and Aubrey received one on behalf of Arthur Shrewsbury, who had made thirty-five 'and in the course of a very brief speech returned thanks for the cordial welcome that had been given to the English cricketers in Brisbane.'

Arthur Coningham, who was later to become part of a very messy and public divorce case, and who once caused a furore at Lord's when lighting a fire in the outfield to warm his hands on a cold day, had made eighteen, and accordingly took the cup for Queensland. The Englishmen had won by ten wickets, and in the second innings Aubrey had dismissed ten for twenty-four or twenty-eight, depending on whether you believe *Wisden* or the *Brisbane Courier*. Somewhat ironically, he had bowled Coningham for a duck when he had batted a second time.

The match finished with storm clouds brewing, and as the eleven took the boat down Moreton Bay en route to Maryborough the thunderstorm broke and the forked lightning made a vivid and spectacular backcloth to a sea swarming with shoals of shark. The steamer dropped anchor to await a favourable tide, and the passengers enjoyed watching the efforts of the crew to haul in white-tips, bonitos, whalers, and a great hammer-head. The sharks won easily as the tally was two caught and seven dropped. For Aubrey it revived disconcerting memories of fishing trips in Sydney. 'While two or three of us, in pyjamas, were standing in three feet of water, we heard a shout, and, turning round, saw a shark between us and the shore – a distance of only five or six yards. He was the wickedest-looking being I ever saw. Fortunately, he was frightened at the noise, and bolted. One Sunday morning we were catching fish over in Vaucluse Bay; that is to say, we sat on a rock eating oysters while we fished for schnapper, about the size of a cod. We were hauling one into the boat when a shark came along and nipped him in two. He had the tail and we the head.'

The storm had succeeded in clearing the air, and the match

against Twenty-two of Maryborough commenced in much less oppressive conditions. About twelve hundred people gave themselves a day off work to watch the Englishmen bat unconcernedly for 163, before scuttling the locals for forty-one in only seventy-five minutes, with Briggs and Pougher sharing the twenty-one wickets.

The game was scheduled to last for two days, but although Maryborough provided stiffer opposition in their second knock, they still were unable to avoid an innings defeat. This time it was Aubrey who took the honours with Lohmann, bowling destructively to capture 11 for 14 off 108 balls including the hat-trick. The Englishmen then worked off the somnolifying effects of a splendidly plentiful luncheon provided by Mr A. J. Heap, by entertaining the crowd with an exhibition innings during which C. A. S. opened his shoulders and drove a ball right over the shed at the far end of the ground, thereby causing some embarrassment to a gentleman who was caught *in flagrante delicto* by the retrieving fieldsman as he defecated in what he had thought was comparative privacy.

The next morning the team left by the morning train for Gympie, which was a gold-mining settlement just over a third of the way back to Brisbane. After the usual pleasantries and speech-making, during which the Mayor, Captain Ferguson, announced that the coming of the English cricketers to Gympie had been looked forward to with *mild* interest for several weeks, the Oldfellows band led a procession of buggies and buses to the Mining Exchange Hotel for some light refreshment. Suitably replenished, Aubrey retaliated by saying that he wished the Gympie team success in a *general* sort of way in the future, whereupon the assembled company all retired to Queen's Park where Gympie Twenty-two went in to bat. There was no safety to be found in numbers as the twenty-two promptly formed a sorry procession back to the pavilion (a grandiose term for what was no more than a large *messoige*) routed for forty-five, with over half of the runs coming from only two batsmen. Every single one of the English side was then keen to bat early in the order, as it was obvious that Gympie were completely outclassed, and that on a small ground there were runs for the taking, even though the opposition had so many bodies in the field. Aubrey, displaying considerable diplomacy, decided to draw lots for the privilege, and perhaps as a reward for his having taken thirteen wickets Fate promoted Johnny Briggs to open the innings. With George Lohmann indisposed and unable to bat, all but one of the remaining ten Englishmen reached double figures, with Aubrey gallantly ignoring his lot placing by going in last, making a hard hitting forty-nine in very quick time. The game was now in its second day, and Gympie never remotely looked like making the Englishmen bat again as they struggled to seventy-nine with C. A. S. dismissing 5 for 20.

Gympie was an inland township, and therefore the most practicable way back to Brisbane was to journey north once more to Maryborough and catch the steamer. A special train was provided for the team, and after two and a half hours of rhythmic jolting they reached Maryborough Station at 11 p.m., where they renewed acquaintance with the local cricketers who had thoughtfully laid on an oyster supper.

The boat left at five the next morning, though most of the cricketers found their berths in the early hours and tried to catch what sleep they could. The voyage was stormless and uneventful, and now there was to be four days respite before they took on Eighteen of Queensland once again.

Encouraged by the kindly cajoling of irascible editors, the local press began ferreting for any possible morsel of news that would assume greater magnitude by being connected to the impressive English tourists, and so breakfasting Brisbanians learned that 'the members of the world-famed brotherhood of Smith will be glad to hear that the Captain of Shrewsbury's eleven is not the only one of the distinguished family in the Colonies capable of acquitting himself with credit on the cricket field. The Sydney Referee is my authority for the intelligence that eleven Smiths played eleven of the Manly Club a few weeks ago and as was only to be expected came out of the fray with flying colours, beating the Manly – perish the thought that the Smiths are unmanly – by fifty-three runs on the first innings. The critic of the Referee seems quite hurt that the Smiths are developing so rapidly in the Colonies, but he hardly appreciates the inexhaustible resources of the tribe, "This is about the first team of brothers or namesakes," says the

Referee, "that has shown itself out in the colony, but in England the Christopherson Bros are reckoned a very formidable team. We are getting more like England every day, but bother it all, there are too many Smiths in and around Manly." ' A number of batsmen in that Australian summer found that even one Smith was far too many.

Brisbane was stiflingly hot and several of the side who had under-estimated the power of the sun were suffering from heat exhaustion; however, after two such easy victories against undemanding opposition, Aubrey thought that the team needed tuning up before coming to grips with the Queenslanders again. Accordingly, he arranged an exhibition match between an eleven captained by himself, and another captained by Mr L. C. Docker. Each side included local club members to make the required number, and an exciting two day match ended with a victory for Mr Docker's eleven by one wicket. Obviously the match practices were effective, as Queensland were dispatched with relative comfort in spite of their old adversary Coninghan's efforts with the ball.

The match attendance was a great disappointment. At no time were there more than twelve hundred present, and as the game ended hardly fifty souls could be seen. Even the presence of the august Governor provided small consolation, and undoubtedly it was a promotional mistake to play two games against Queensland within such a short time span. Australians do not relish seeing their side being comprehensively beaten, and after the first defeat by ten wickets the odds were stacked heavily against the home team.

It was back to boat again for the return to Sydney, and though by now all of the team were hardened sailors, there was general satisfaction at making the thirty-eight hour passage under a cloudless sky and over a waveless sea. The following day in Sydney the weather was not so kind. There was a gale-force wind from the south-west which blew acrid dust into every cranny and orifice both inanimate and human, and caused net practice to be accompanied by a continuous rubbing of eyes and gasping for breath. However uncomfortable the conditions were, though, it was necessary to be in perfect trim for the return match against New South Wales, and Aubrey had no trouble in keeping the team hard at work, as they were all absolutely determined to avenge the one defeat of their tour.

On Friday, December 9th, in front of a three thousand crowd, M'Donnell, the N.S.W. captain, won the toss and had no hesitation in deciding to bat, no doubt remembering that recently on a very similar wicket his side had accrued 408 against the other tourists from England under G. F. Vernon. The feeling in the Aussie camp was that around 300 would be an acceptable total on such a good wicket, and so Aubrey made up his mind to try and offset the loss of the toss, and restrict the expected heavy scoring, by shuffling the bowlers frequently, thereby keeping them fresh. He used six bowlers, including himself for practically the first time in an opening innings on the tour, and New South Wales never really looked like establishing a reasonable score. If it had not been for Moses, who went in first wicket down and remained undefeated with 78, they would not even have reached three figures.

Faced with a total of 149, Shrewsbury's team started well enough with Shrewsbury himself making 48, but then the middle order fell cheaply and by the time Aubrey came in to join the Lancastrian Johnny Briggs, at 141 for 7, any hopes for a large first innings lead seemed to have been dissipated. The *Sydney Morning Herald* takes up the story:

Now came the stand of the day ... the score mounted with ominous dispatch as many fine drives and cuts reached the fence ... At 3.15, 200 appeared amidst great applause, runs still coming rapidly. Turner took another turn which resulted in Briggs being caught at the wicket from a bad wide off ball. 83 runs had been added during the partnership (seven for 224) ... Smith then drove Ferris grandly to the off over the fence. Runs were still piled on freely, and with his score at 62, Smith was missed by Moses at long off – a difficult running catch. At four o'clock a brief adjournment took place for refreshments, the score then standing at 250, Smith being 68. Soon after, a shout of delight went up from thousands, when Smith's bails were sent flying by Turner, he pulling it on. Never perhaps, had the captain played such a sterling game before; from the commencement he had the bowling apparently at his mercy. Just at the time he went to the wickets, the game certainly looked gloomy for the

English side, but by the plucky game played by him and Briggs, the substantial lead of the visitors was achieved.

Other papers were equally eulogistic, observing that the team had obviously been very handicapped by having to play the first match against N.S.W. without their captain, and noting that despite his ungraceful, angular stance at the wicket, his cutting and driving were as free and fluent as could be desired.

New South Wales batted a second time 130 behind and fared little better, leaving the tourists with but thirty-six to make for a comfortable ten wicket win.

There was much gnashing of teeth and pontification in the press regarding New South Wales' poor performance and in particular M'Donnell's handling of the side. 'Why wasn't Evans bowled?' 'Why pick Tom Garrett who does nothing with the ball, his batting is as weak as a lemon squash, and whose fielding would disgrace a schoolboys' eleven?', and so on *ad nauseam.*

The overall attendance had been rather less than was expected, although ten thousand had turned up on the Saturday in spite of the counter attractions of a Monster Sheffield Handicap at Botany. Among those who had attended the cricket were some who found nothing wrong at all with Aubrey's stance.

I feel sorry for Percy M'Donnell, or rather I was envious of Smith, the captain of the winning team. It is a proud thing to captain a team of cricketers that win an important match. On every hand there are ladies anxious to congratulate and flatter you. It makes one feel like the warriors of old that only the brave deserve the fair. On Monday the English captain had a happy time of it in the grandstand endeavouring to get a word in edgeways among half a score of ladies. Ah! Fickle woman! How lavish were these ladies in their congratulations which they showered without mercy on 'Dear Mr Smith'. I do envy those Englishmen, and I will tell my readers that these self-same ladies but a few weeks ago, or so many days back, were even still more pronounced in exalting over the proud laurels so gloriously won by our boys.

In that way did the Nigel Dempster of the time pass on his soft scoops to the sensation seekers of Sydney. By the time they had read the tittle-tattle, Aubrey and the team were safely ensconced on the 5.15 p.m. Wednesday express to Melbourne for the game against Victoria. Actually they were not all that safe, as one of the sleeping cars caught fire near Goulbourn, and had to be replaced, which meant that the train did not arrive in the spacious metropolis until noon the next day.

Melbourne was in the middle of a boom period that saw its population doubled by immigration to half a million in the space of ten years. The seventh city of the Empire was larger than most European capitals, and in Frank Crowley's *A New History of Australia* it is described as containing stately public buildings and coffee palaces built in indiscriminate styles, with cable trams gliding efficiently through the dense horse-drawn and pedestrian traffic, and three hundred trains a day leaving for the southern and eastern suburbs. Yet at night hundreds of stinking nightcarts disposed of the city's sewage, some 'cutting their journies short by depositing their loads in the streets', and causing typhoid to be rife. Shrewsbury's team were soon aware that the label 'Marvellous Smellbourne' was fully justified.

They also were soon well aware that they were less than welcome. Six of the leading Victorian players found pressing reasons to explain why they were unable to take part in the match, none of the officials of either the Victorian Cricket Association or the Melbourne Club were present to greet the visitors at the hotel or the ground, nobody guided the players around the pavilion or enclosures, at luncheon on all three days of the match Aubrey and his players had to fend for themselves and look around for chairs and places to sit, on an evening visit to the Princess Theatre the Englishmen were left hostless, and to cap it all, there was a snobbish smear campaign started which referred to Vernon's team as 'The Gentlemen of England' thereby inferring that Shrewsbury's were less than that, and moreover that the amateurs in his side were receiving extravagant payments as 'expenses'.

It was painfully obvious that the visit to Melbourne, the home of the sponsors of the rival England team under Vernon, had brought the ill-feeling caused by the two tours to a head.

After the match was over *The Leader* devoted two columns to the discourtesy shown Mr Smith and his men, castigating petty officialdom for allowing a promotional quarrel to fall on the heads of those who had nothing to do with it. Not that that was of any help to the Englishmen during the course of an uncomfortable stay.

In fact, it was not until Charley Beal from the Sydney Association arrived to watch the game, realised what was going on, and then literally dragged the pompous 'Majah' Wardill, who was the Melbourne C.C. secretary, to meet Aubrey that there was anything remotely approaching normal relations.

The Victorian side minus most of their star players, including Spofforth, was painfully weak, and soon capitulated for a meagre sixty-eight. The English side then proceeded to amass the monumental total of 624 with Arthur Shrewsbury batting superbly for a double century, and George Brann making an excellent 118. Nearly everybody scored profusely, though Aubrey did not linger long with a duck and, of course, with so many runs accumulated it was immaterial. The Victorians managed to do little better in their second knock, and were all out for a tidy hundred, and so the winning margin was an extraordinary one innings and 456 runs.

During the English innings another unfortunate episode had occurred. Hastings, the Victorian stumper, became unwell and had to leave the field, to be followed shortly by M'Shane, their number three bat, who took himself off to play in a second class Cup game between North Melbourne and Fitzroy, apparently under the conviction that in this fixture at least club came before colony. Boyle, the Victorian captain, quickly approached several prominent players who were watching from the pavilion, and asked if they would field as substitutes. All of them refused to do so. The harassed and unhappy captain then was left with no alternative but to approach Aubrey and request two fielders from the opposing side. Though expressing some surprise, the English captain agreed readily enough and so he and Maurice Read took the field as volunteer Victorians.

From the Melbourne C.C.'s point of view, it had not helped to have the final stages of this sorry saga witnessed by the New South Wales players who had just arrived at the ground. There was widespread disapproval of M'Shane's action (partly condoned when it was learned later that he had warned his captain well in advance of his intentions and had arranged, so he thought, his own substitute from amongst the spectating players), and of the attitude of some of the members, and it was yet another of the disagreeable incidents that marred the visit to the city, and helped keep alight the flames of controversy for a long while to come.

For the most part, Aubrey managed to stay aloof from the dissension, and it was left to Lohmann and Docker to percolate news of the pantomime to the local press. Some newspaper editors chose to ignore the facts, though the reaction generally was disgust at the way the English tourists had been treated, and sympathy for what they had had to put up with. Perhaps less predictably, those feelings were echoed by Vernon's men, who after all had been sponsored by the very people who had caused the trouble.

As if all this had not been enough, the unhappy stay in Melbourne was capped by an accident in practice that involved players from both the English camps. In one net, the popular Yorkshireman Billy Bates from Vernon's group was bowling to Blackham, and in another Newham was facing George Brann, both of whom, of course, were amateur team-mates of Aubrey's at Sussex, and in the Shrewsbury, Shaw, Lillywhite party. Just as Bates began his run-up, Newham hit a tremendous drive which caught the unfortunate Yorkshireman with full force under the right eye, and not only put him out of the Vernon tour but effectively finished his career in first class cricket for ever.

After a week's rest, during which feelings became only fractionally less ruffled, Shrewsbury's side journeyed to the gold fields once more to begin a match against Twenty-two of Ballarat at the Eastern Oval on Christmas Eve. Aubrey won the toss, put the locals in on a drying wicket and proceeded to take 5 for 11, assisted mainly by Joe Preston of Yorkshire who had even better figures with 7 for 22. The eight wicket victory by the visitors was practically a foregone conclusion.

New Year's Eve saw the start of a drawn game against Eighteen of Bendigo at Sandhurst, and on the Sunday, which was New Year's Day, half of the team were driven fifteen miles into the outback to shoot rabbit. Apparently they killed over two hundred, and it was only the enervating heat encouraging an early ceasefire that saved many more from being slaughtered.

On the return to Melbourne the Englishmen were involved in another drawn game, this time against Eighteen Melbourne Juniors, who were precocious enough to ignore reputations by leading comfortably on the first innings. Aubrey trundled in his usual inexpensive fashion for a few overs, and there was a comment in a Victorian newspaper to the effect that C. A. Smith did not bowl himself enough. The critic pointed out that when Aubrey did go on, he was nearly always successful, and opined that he was a better bowler than some of those used more frequently. It is not likely that Aubrey would have paid much attention to the remarks, though in the next match his opponents would have found that hard to believe.

Bowral was on the main line between Melbourne and Sydney, about eighty miles from the New South Wales capital. With its relatively temperate climate, guaranteeing cool nights, it was fast becoming a fashionable resort for many who worked in the city. The cricket ground lay picturesquely at the foot of a hill and the groundsman obviously felt that to cut the grass would not enhance the scenic beauty. The wicket was a matting one, and the outfield was not only unmown and lumpy but ankle deep in cow dung. The antics of the fielders trying to avoid the perils underfoot made up in entertainment for what the cricket lacked with its poor standard.

Aubrey opened the batting with George Lohmann, and with a mixture of caution and vigorous hitting managed twenty-nine before being caught at the wicket. Of the rest of the side only Ulyett, Briggs and Newham achieved double figures with the result that the English Eleven were all out for 126. Bowral collapsed for forty-two to the bowling of Briggs and Lohmann, and when following on did little better, as Aubrey took 9 for 15 and Pougher 8 for 25. Superficially the innings defeat of Bowral augured well for the eagerly awaited rubber match against New South Wales, though every knowing person was only too aware that the opposition and conditions would be totally different this time.

Perhaps the fact that the match started on Friday the 13th

boded ill for the tourists. Although Lohmann bowled the side into a good position on the first morning they were never really in the hunt thereafter, and the batting for New South Wales of Moses, who made a fifty and a century, and the bowling of Turner, who had match figures of 16 for 79, proved decisive. Apart from Shrewsbury and Newham, the Englishmen batted badly and suffered the second defeat of their tour by the margin of 153 runs, which inevitably led to considerable rejoicing throughout the colony.

There is nothing like a twenty-two hour train journey in which to find ample time to post-mortemise on such a depressing loss, and already low spirits plummeted to zero when the visitors realised that the famous Zig-Zag in the Blue Mountains would pass unseen with a traversal at night. The cricketers were aiming for Bourke, five hundred miles into the interior from Sydney, and according to the local scribes it was the first time that any English team had travelled so far inland. The preparations for the visit had been going on for weeks, the racecourse had been requisitioned, and many hours had been spent pushing a roller back and forth to gain a reasonably even surface on which to lay stretched green matting. There had even been attention paid to the surrounding area, though it still managed to resemble a well-ploughed and harrowed seed field. The *pièce de résistance*, however, had come when the locals had set fire to the ungovernable scrub, which meant that the whole ground was coated in white ash; consequently a ball from even a fast-medium bowler would stop nearly dead on pitching.

After their exhausting journey the tourists' arrival at 6.00 p.m. had been greeted exuberantly by practically the whole populace, who determinedly led the way to a noisy and bibulous reception that staggered on into the small hours. The remainder of the night was spent lying on the hotel verandah in order to try and catch what little air was still circulating. Little wonder that next day in a furnace temperature of 117°F a decidedly bleary, jaded English team made feeble batting motions rather than score any runs against twenty-two stalwarts from Bourke. By mid-afternoon the tourists were all out for a paltry sixty-nine, and accordingly took their turn making moonscape footprints across the field in the oven-like heat.

Bourke eventually succumbed for 104, and Aubrey had the distinction of taking 7 for 8, six of whom were clean bowled.

The following day the match petered out into a draw, nobody feeling much inclined to prolong proceedings in such a climate. The hospitable hosts presented Briggs with a fiver for getting top score in the match, and Mr Newham with a pair of carefully mounted emu eggs for the highest knock in the first innings. A thoughtful gesture which relieved the amateur of any possible embarrassment at having to be seen accepting such a sordid item as actual cash.

Sunday was reserved for rest and recreation, and most of the team caught up with lost sleep under the weeping willows on the Darling River, and then, with energy restored, opted to join a wild turkey shoot on the Monday.

There were a further four days' respite before the next match, and it was an opportunity for Aubrey to become acquainted with the interim financial position of the tour from Lillywhite and Shrewsbury. It was not good, but it could have been worse. Attendances, whilst occasionally excellent, had been mostly very disappointing, though, with the remainder of the tour concentrated on more heavily populated townships, there were hopes that the promoters might still emerge with a small profit, or at least break even. There was a certain wicked satisfaction in learning that the Melbourne authorities who had treated them so badly were heavily in debt with Vernon's tour.

It was now late January, and during the next six weeks the team played eight matches to conclude the Australian part of their tour. From the playing point of view it was a highly successful period. There was an easy innings victory over twenty-two Men of Orange during which Aubrey took 3 for 10; a five-wicket defeat of a Combined Australian XI, which comprised an amalgam of the Victorian and New South Wales players, and in this match Aubrey distinguished himself by being unluckily run out off a rebound at the bowler's end, and also dropping two catches, one easy, one difficult, an almost unheard of event that attracted a lot of ribald comment. For several months the Australian press had been speculating on a rubber match between the two English touring sides, and this had aroused the promotional instincts of Shaw, Shrewsbury

and Lillywhite who had actively encouraged such an encounter. Vernon's team, however, fought shy of the gambits, no
doubt fearing a defeat, and excused themselves with talk of a
heavy schedule. The compromise was for the two teams to join
forces against Australia, although this had been mooted as an
entirely separate venture as well. The match now took place in
Sydney with Walter Read as captain (neither Aubrey or
George Vernon played), and resulted in an impressive win for
the English.

For Shaw, Shrewsbury and Lillywhite's clients a drawn
game with eighteen able cricketers from Newcastle followed,
and C.A.S. rediscovered his catching form by snapping up
three in the slips. He also mopped up the Newcastle tail in
their first innings with 3 for 5, and then took four wickets in the
second, and not six, as is given erroneously in some newspaper
reports and in *Wisden*. It was George Lohmann who had the
distinction of taking six wickets and not four.

Around this time the tourists' enforced love affair with the
Australian railways was strained to the limit. The journey to
Newcastle had to be broken two hours out from Sydney at
Hawksbury because the building of a bridge was incomplete,
and so passengers and baggage were transferred to a steam
launch for a five mile ferry up river before they could join
another train and the finished section of the line. Then, just in
case disaffection had not finally arrived, the excursion to
Tamworth from Newcastle, which was less than two hundred
miles, took thirteen and a half hours at an average speed of
about fourteen miles per hour. Remarkably, in his response to
the hearty toasts and cheers at the reception, Aubrey was still
benignly optimistic. 'Certainly no body of men are more
pleased than we are in reaching Tamworth after such a long,
tiresome journey; that, however, will soon be forgotten in the
memory of such kindness as we have all just received from the
citizens and sportsmen of the town.'

Displaying the resilience of conditioned travellers, Aubrey
and his men proceeded to give Tamworth a nine wicket
drubbing, and then returned to Sydney to demoralise the Sixth
Australian team, who were shortly to depart for England, with
a brilliant innings victory. Eighteen Sydney Juniors emulated
their Victorian counterparts by holding the tourists to a draw

over three days, and then Eighteen of Bathurst emulated many
of their countrymen in the preceding months by being defeated
comprehensively in two. Aubrey took seven wickets in the first
innings of this match.

The return game against the Sixth Australian team in
Sydney begun on the 9th of March brought the gruelling trip to
Australia to a triumphant close. Aubrey won the toss and
elected to bat. It was the obvious choice on a hard wicket and
in fine weather; however, there were signs that this would
disintegrate under an ominous-looking cloud bank in the
south-east, which for the moment was being held at bay by a
strong breeze. At 98 for 6 the tourists' first innings appeared to
be folding for an easily accessible total when Aubrey joined the
Warwickshire amateur Docker and began to bat in his usual
positive fashion. With two fiercely struck fours he removed
Ferris from the attack and quickly altered the whole complexion of the game. He continued to find the boundary with some
frequency, and was not afraid to hit the ball in the air; there
was never a moment, though, when he gave the semblance of a
chance. It was not until the score had reached 201 with only
Pougher to come in that he pressed too hard and was caught by
the persevering Turner off his own bowling. Aubrey had
provided the cliché writers with their 'captain's innings' and
was cheered back to the pavilion for his dramatic and
invaluable fifty-nine.

The Australians were indebted to Blackham when they went
in, and at the halfway stage they were only twenty-two behind.
From then on it was really Shrewsbury's match. He batted
magnificently in the second innings for a double century, ably
supported by Aubrey, who this time took a more restrained
rôle for his forty. During the course of his knock Aubrey had to
suffer a nasty blow in the mouth whilst attempting a forward
lunge to a ball outside the off stump. The ball had found the
top of the bat and been deflected too rapidly to be avoided.
Fortunately, the damage appeared slight and after a pause for
repairs Aubrey continued batting. Nevertheless, he must have
been shaken, and was out soon afterwards. Even with a century
from their opening bat, Jones, the Australians never came
within striking distance of the English effort, and were
defeated by 158 runs.

It was time now for fond farewells to the veritable host of admirers and friends that had been gained during the trip. Most of the team were proceeding to New Zealand for a short tour before beginning the long voyage home, though Mr Docker was staying in Australia for a month or so in order to transact some business. The Union Company's steamship *Hantoro* left Sydney Harbour at 10.00 p.m. on Saturday, 17th March, with the cricketers aboard, and they were cheered on their way by a large assembly gathered on the quay. The last few days had seen a seemingly endless round of celebratory parties, only interrupted by a few snatched moments in an attempt to pack what appeared to be at least twice the amount of luggage that they had started out with. Whatever remained of their energies had been largely dissipated with the dregs in the glasses, though on clearing the Heads they found an unpleasant sting in the tail which dealt an irresistible *coup de grâce*. A strong southerly wind blew a three-day storm, and it was a case of heard but not seen for three-quarters of the party. The wind changed to westerly as they were going through Cook Strait, and it was with profound relief and faltering step that the majority disembarked at Wellington on the Thursday afternoon to be met by their hosts from the North Island.

The start of the game against Wellington had been delayed one day owing to the late arrival of the boat, and when the Englishmen took the train to the gates of the ground next morning it was raining steadily, which seemed to point to a further postponement. Luckily the clouds cleared quickly, and the tourists made an entertaining 207 in just over three hours before a crowd of over two thousand, which the *Sporting Life* informs us 'included many ladies'. Bad light brought an early close to play with Wellington having lost seventeen wickets in making seventy-one.

On the Saturday the home side were forced to follow on after adding a further fifteen runs. In their second innings they shaped better. 'The Englishmen put on two fresh bowlers, Mr Smith and Mr Preston, the former being particularly formidable with his fast yorkers, and with his strong leg-break, thirteen of the wickets falling before him for the small number of 30 runs. He secured the first nine wickets, all of them clean bowled.' Unless Wellington batted out of order, it would appear from the scorecard that the first *eight* victims were clean bowled, though in all Aubrey hit the stumps in eleven of his thirteen dismissals. His final tally was 13 for 36 from 34.3 overs with twenty-two maidens.

Sunday was spent at sea again on the steamer to Christ-church, where the tourists were due to take on Eighteen of Canterbury at Lancaster Park the following day. Rain seriously interfered with the match and it finished as an unsatisfactory draw. Aubrey acquired three wickets and two catches, and on several occasions during the course of the Canterbury innings found it necessary to urge his fielders to 'back up' in no uncertain voice. With the end of the tour in sight, and in the bitter cold of a windswept day, it was not surprising to find slackness creeping into the play. As the weather had been so bad, the Canterbury authorities generously offered to play another two-day game against the Englishmen with all the proceeds going as a complimentary benefit to the visitors. The fixture was scheduled for the Friday and Saturday of departure at Hagley Park, and this time Jupiter Pluvius decided to be kind. The tourists had much the better of a draw, with Briggs and Lohmann getting most of the wickets, and as soon as the game ended there was a hurried departure to the hotel before making the half-hour trip to Port Lyttleton to board ship for the voyage home. Promptly at seven o'clock on 31st March, the *Coptic* began wending its way into the Pacific Ocean for Rio de Janeiro and eventually Plymouth. Ten weary cricketers (they had said goodbye to Shrewsbury and Lillywhite, who had stayed behind to organise a football tour) settled down for a six-week respite before facing once again the realities and responsibilities of their life at home.

The playing and social side of the Antipodean tour had been rewarding and successful, excepting of course the Melbourne episode. Of twenty-five matches played, fourteen had been won, nine drawn (mostly ending with the tourists in command), and only two lost. Aubrey had proved an enormously popular and able captain both on and off the field. Early on during the trip he had turned to his senior professionals, particularly Shrewsbury, for advice on field placing, but as the tour progressed so did his confidence in his own judgement. 'He had appealed to all classes,' was the magazine *Cricket's* rather condescending and snobbish summary. In all matches on the tour Aubrey had scored 442 runs, often when they were most needed, and taken over a hundred wickets. If he had not been so modestly disinclined to display his skill with the ball more often, undoubtedly the total would have soared even higher. Obviously there were a multitude of cheap wickets available, with the simultaneous tours necessitating the playing of so many games in the poorly equipped outback, and it was equally obvious that neither party stood much chance of making a profit in the circumstances. The deficit on Shaw, Shrewsbury and Lillywhite's venture was around £1500, and on Vernon's tour the Melbourne authorities lost nearly £4000. Aggravation at the situation was compounded when the local press published details of the *amateur* Walter Read's expenses. They came to £1137.10s. The professionals earned from £220 to £300 each! In the same paragraph, it was noted that whilst in the South Island, New Zealand, the amateurs in Lillywhite's team (including, of course, Aubrey) were put up at the Christchurch Club at Lillywhite's expense, whereas the professionals stayed at the White Hart Hotel. The report does acknowledge that the pros were most comfortable there. Ah, consciences assuaged! 'Twas ever thus, and it took cricket a further seventy years or so to end the distinction.

Since well before Christmas past, Shaw, Shrewsbury and Lillywhite had realised that they were likely to have to sustain a financial loss over the tour, and naturally enough had been thinking of ways to recoup the balance. The idea of a football tour for the Australian winter had been aired and thought viable, and whilst Alfred Shaw had been at home in England organising a side to make the trip, Shrewsbury and Lillywhite, when not playing cricket, had been busily arranging a possible fixture list. They had approached also the three Sussex amateurs in the cricket side, Brann, Newham and Aubrey, who had turned out several times for the County F.A., with a view to them staying on in Australia to be part of the football tour. Not surprisingly news of the offer, and the possibility of Sussex C.C.C. being without three of their stalwarts for the coming season, had filtered through to the sports pages in England, and caused some despondency amongst cricket supporters. Aubrey had written home to test the parental view, and his father's reaction eventually became public knowledge through a published letter written in forthright terms to the editor of the *Sporting Life:*

> Sir,
>   Your reporter repeats a statement which has more than once appeared, as to my son remaining in Australia to play football, and this morning states that Shaw 'is inclined to think that Mr Brann and Mr Smith will remain, &c'. When the football business was first mooted my son wrote home asking if I objected to his remaining. He said I was to write at once to Shaw, who would cable my reply. I wrote asking Shaw to cable a decided negative to his staying. From a cablegram which appeared a month later I fancied Shaw could not have cabled. I therefore wrote him on the subject. He replied that he had not cabled as he thought a letter would be all that was necessary, he also said he was glad that I had decided against my son's remaining. I again wrote Shaw, and told him that in the event of my son having made any arrangement to stay he would have to break it, and the blame would rest with Shaw. In every letter I have written to my son since the question first arose I have urged his returning to England.
>
> Yours &c   CHARLES J. SMITH
> 12, Great St. Helens, E.C.

The letter is an interesting insight into Victorian paternalism, and in particular Aubrey's relationship with his father. It is revealing to find that even though Aubrey had had far more independence, acclaim and authority than most other twenty-four-year-olds of his time, he was still very much beholden to the pater's wishes, if not purse strings. One must also not discount the possibility that after nearly eight months away Aubrey was not keen on remaining to play football and, therefore suggested that his father make a negative reply through Shaw, as a convenient method of saving any hurt feelings or embarrassment that might come from a direct refusal himself.

If there was still any doubt in England as to whether Aubrey

would be staying, it was dispelled when a letter from George
Brann to a friend in Brighton arrived in mid-April:

> I thought you would like to know whether I intend staying
> out here with the football team, as I see it is reported that
> Mr Smith and self are going to do so. We have now both
> made up our minds to come home ... Mr Smith played
> awfully well, and will, next season, make a lot of runs if he
> keeps up his form.

4/From Sussex to South Africa

The rigours and excitements of Australia soon receded in the memory as Aubrey flung himself into the task of trying to meld the Sussex side into a successful and combative unit for the 1888 season. The realities of the county circuit again were soon apparent; few easy pickings as in the Antipodes, and even if Aubrey did play 'awfully well' and achieve his best all-round season in the first-class game, it was mostly with the ball that he had his triumphs. Not, though, in the first game of the season against Grace's Gloucestershire. There he batted with truly Bothamesque bravura.

'When Jesse Hide was joined by Mr Smith, the total was 104 for five wickets. These two then obtained a thorough mastery over the bowling and hit with really remarkable freedom. They put on 161 runs in an hour and forty minutes and completely altered the aspect of the game – Mr Smith gave two chances at 38 and 51 but he nevertheless deserves great praise for his 85 in which there were eleven 4's, three 3's, and eight 2's.' (*Wisden*)

The feat inspired verses which might easily have come from the pen of Albert Craig, 'Cricket Rhymster'. One read:—

To praise in simple well-meant rhyme
The Sussex men I've tried,
All praise to gallant Captain Smith,
And good old Jesse Hide,
It matters not who'er you meet,
You never falter till you're beat.

Even though Aubrey took 5 for 49 in the second innings and

with Arthur Hide caused a Gloucestershire collapse, the game finished as a draw. Gloucestershire's first innings total of 428, dominated by a W.G. double century, ensured safety, though it was a far from discouraging start to the season for the Sussex side.

A few days later Aubrey took himself off to Lord's, and replenished his desire for victims 'down under' by capturing four of the visiting Australians for the Gentlemen. It was to be the first of seven encounters with the Australians that summer, in the company of six different teams. It was another drawn game, as became likely when the match was limited to two days because of the running of the Derby on the third.

Aubrey was not in the least tempted by the colourful exodus of the racegoers to Epsom, as he had to take the train north to rejoin his Sussex team in Manchester. And how thankful they were that he was with them. 7 for 59 in Lancashire's first innings, and ten wickets in the match. It was not enough though to gain a result.

The Lancashire fixture was the start of a three-match northern tour for Sussex, in which they lost by 116 runs to Yorkshire at Sheffield, and beat Durham by 237 runs in a friendly at Sunderland. Then followed a spell of three dispiriting defeats at home in Brighton. As Aubrey himself recalled in a letter nearly sixty years later, 'Sussex in my time lacked the batting power, which came along with Charles Fry and Ranji.'

The annual skirmish between the Gents and Players at Lord's at the end of the first week of July brought not only one of the outstanding moments of his entire career for Aubrey but also perhaps the most exciting and startling finish in the history of the fixture.

In the Players' first innings Aubrey had taken 3 for 23 in 23 overs, his victims comprising Abel, Gunn and Attewell. Accurate bowling in any circumstances, but as the game reached the home turn the Players needed a mere seventy-eight to win. They reached 70 for 6, with many of the crowd having left the terraces, and only a few stalwarts still supporting the Tavern. W. G. Grace had sunk into his familiar crouch at point when *Wisden* reports that, 'as a last resource Steel handed the ball to Smith at 71, and this proved the turning-point of the game.' Aubrey described the ensuing events in an epistle to the editor of the *Cricketer* published in the Annual of 1943/4.

One run was added ... 6 to make and 4 to go. Then with the last ball of the over, I got Attewell with one that went 'up the hill' (Aubrey was bowling from the Nursery End or Orchard End as he liked to refer to it) – surprisingly to me, I felt it must have pitched on a heel mark.

6 to make and 3 to go.

With the last ball of Sammy's (Woods) next over he got Bobby Peel with an 'off-bailer'.

6 to make and 2 to go.

George Lohmann had a swipe at my second ball – and he went back (L.B.W.)

6 to make and 1 to go.

Mordecai Sherwin took Lohmann's place; I tried him with a yorker. I tried him with a second yorker and then with a swinger, but devil a bit, Mordecai's bat was as still as the stumps. We both grinned at each other as over was called. I turned back and remarked to Wilfred Flowers: 'Mordy seems all right.' To which Flowers replied: 'Yes sir, he's like me, he takes a deal of frightening.' Then I noticed he was as green as grass! The first ball from Sammy was a half volley. Flowers was a week late at it and away went his middle stump. We had won by 5 runs.

It was a cue for the crowd to surge on to the pitch and gather in front of the pavilion calling for the two heroes, who eventually appeared and somewhat bashfully acknowledged the plaudits.

The Players extracted considerable revenge in the subsequent match at the Oval when they won by an innings, but Aubrey's part in that memorable victory at Lord's was still being talked about ten days later, when the Australian tourists visited the South Coast and lost a memorable and low-scoring battle to Sussex by fifty-eight runs. In this game his contribution was less noticeable, with one exception:— 'I shall never forget when I caught the famous Trott. He hit the ball high into the air. I was fielding at cover point, and I thought the ball would never come down. It whirled around and round. I could see the ball and thousands of pairs of eyes watching me. You will see that I caught it – what a relief.'

The victory for Sussex was made even sweeter by being so unexpected. Craig, who used to tour the grounds of Southern England and sell his rhymes for a penny a sheet, was present, and equal to the occasion:

BRITISH GRIT TRIUMPHANT
Sussex beat Australia at Hove July 20th, 1888
Written on the Ground after the Match

Did you hear that big shout?
It dispels every doubt,
Old Sussex have put the Australians to rout.
Our 'Cracks' struggled on
Till the conflict was won,
What Surrey had failed to do, Sussex has done.
Captain Smith (honoured name)
Had one object in view,
And his men (gallant hearts) like their captain stood true.
They meant victory – that's it,
And no men are more fit
To show better samples of rare British grit.

The County then needed all the 'grit' they could muster when they experienced a luckless barren period losing four matches in a row, the last against Surrey at the Oval being by the colossal margin of an innings and 485 runs. Surrey's total of 698 runs was then a record innings total for a first-class match in England, and Aubrey's meagre consolation was to top score in both of Sussex's comparatively short stays at the crease.

After such a disastrous defeat it says a lot for the spirit of the side, and also Aubrey's qualities of leadership, that two days later they were able to defeat Lancashire by nine wickets (even though the northeners were without Briggs and Sugg), and then in the fixture against Hampshire emerge as victors by an innings and 63 runs. Aubrey took six wickets in the Hants match, but as *Wisden* relates the Sussex innings was 'chiefly remarkable for the extraordinarily brilliant innings of 142 played by Mr Smith. That gentleman went in when four wickets were down with the score at 59, and was ninth out at 288, having in two hours and fifty minutes made 142 out of the 299 scored. He gave a chance at the wicket when he had made 59, but this was the only fault in his grand innings which consisted of twenty 4's, six 3's, twelve 2's and twenty singles.'

It was his first century in a county match, and very similar to the 'knock' he played for the Gentlemen of Sussex against the visiting Parsees. There he savaged a weak attack for 140 runs in rapid time. The sports reporter of the local 'rag' was inspired enough to write colourful mauve prose, and drew parallels with two other previous centuries by Aubrey, one for St John's and one for Brighton against Eshing.

C. A. S.'s Sussex season finished with the return game against Yorkshire and a splendid analysis of 6 for 37 off twenty-six overs in their first innings. Lord Hawke and Bobby Peel, two old adversaries, were among his haul. A tight game was lost by three wickets.

Sussex had finished last of the eight counties, which was desperately disappointing for both players and supporters, who felt they deserved better. At times they had promised much, and there had been a number of individual displays of cricketing quality, but there was not enough overall strength in the side to compete successfully against the majority of the other counties. Sussex had suffered from the death of F. M. Lucas, the illness of Bean, and the unavailability of F. Thomas, and had been hampered when Aubrey had received an arm injury early in the season which became painful when bowling. *Wisden* in their summary of the season made it clear that 'on several occasions the team were overmatched, but more than once a really fine finish was brought about, and the losers deserved almost as much credit as the victors ... We should think ... that, amateurs and professionals alike, the Sussex men found a great deal of pleasure in fighting the battles of their county under so keen and energetic a captain as Mr C. A. Smith.'

In September there were two games for Aubrey against the Aussies for Shrewsbury's team at Leeds and Manchester, both won, and a final turn out at the Hastings Festival for South of England against, surprisingly, the Australians yet again. This was the only game that C. A. S. had played in against the Aussies throughout the season, that was lost. However, he managed forty-four in the first innings.

There were now only two months to go before Aubrey embarked on the trip that was not only significant historically for cricket, but significant personally for him in a way that could not be foreseen.

Before that, however, there were Sussex Football Association meetings to attend, presided over by his father; games for the County against London in which his right wing runs caused havoc in the opposing defence, and an appearance for the Swifts against the Canadians at the Oval which was followed by a presentation to the Prince of Wales.

The weeks passed quickly. The Land of Golden Opportunity beckoned ...

The environs of the East India Dock at Blackwall in the late autumn of 1888 were not the most salubrious or safest of places to be. On the east of the basin lay the dingy Rising Sun, and to the north and south an unruly patchwork of scruffy lodging houses, screaming infants, pilots' pubs, free fights and stinking Thames, all competing as if for focal points on a Gustave Doré engraving. And on the west lay the Whitechapel murders barely cold, with the last in the horrific cycle less than two weeks old. The sight of the dismembered remains of the luckless ladies of the night still held the East End of London in a state of shock and alarm, with the populace unaware that Montague Druitt, who may have been the Ripper, was shortly to be found floating in that same unsavoury Thames. Druitt was a cricketer, and so were many of the hundred guests wending their way to luncheon on board the Royal Mail steamer the *Garth Castle* at the request of Sir Donald Currie, who was a wealthy businessman, founder of a shipping line and patron of the game. The new Hastie cabs with the inflammable lamp, ivory fittings and speaking tubes, rattled into the Ripperies and discharged their distinguished occupants through the self-acting doors on to the dockside in front of a gawping urchinhood, and then beat very 'hastie' retreats.

This luncheon to send off the first officially organised visit to South Africa by a cricketing side representing England marked the start of a merry-go-round of hospitality – balls, concerts, dinners, displays, socialising of every kind that was to last throughout the four and a half month trip. The publicity surrounding the tour was to be continuous and considerable as well, with every insubstantial and inconsequential happening remarked upon and written about in great detail.

The trip was the brainchild of Major R. Gardner Warton, who had been on the General Staff of the Army in South Africa for five years from 1883. He also had played a few games for Essex in his time, and though he was described as honorary secretary for the tour, his function was more that of manager. Aubrey was captain, and the rest of the side was a democratic division of six amateurs and six professionals. M. P. Bowden (Surrey). B. A. F. Grieve (Harrow), E. McMaster (Eton and Cambridge), Hon. C. Coventry (Eton), A. C. Skinner, and J. Roberts, a Freshman at Cambridge, all spoke the Queen's English and provided the social distinctions necessary for acceptance of adventurous yet fallible performance by some of them on the field of play. The hard core of the team was to be found in the reliable professionalism of Johnny Briggs (Lancashire), who had toured with Aubrey in Australia, Harry Wood, Bobby Abel, and Maurice Read of Surrey, Frank Hearne of Kent, and A. J. Fothergill of Somerset.

'A day or two ago I saw in a newspaper that we are considered by no means a first class team,' said Aubrey in his reply to the toast proposed by Sir Donald Currie. 'I think that is obviously an unnecessary remark and somewhat unjust to Major Warton. Doubtless if it had been necessary, Major Warton could have got together as strong a combination as ever left the shores of England. But the fact must be borne in mind that we are a pioneer team. No English team has ever before visited South Africa. It would be a very dangerous thing to have effected a very strong combination – just as dangerous as to have a very weak one. (Hear, hear.) If a very strong team goes to South Africa the germs of cricket might be crushed out, each individual might be disappointed, and each club be made to feel itself impotent, as it were. Equal objection might be made to a very weak team. We are anxious to hold our own, and of course we are anxious to have amongst us men who can show what good cricket is – also men of the genuine type seen on county grounds at home, where professionals and amateurs are in sympathetic touch together purifying the game and showing an example to all sportsmen.' (Cheers.)

Purifying the game, indeed! Ah well, it had been a good lunch. Among the sitters were Viscount Oxenbridge, Lord George Scott, and Sir George Baden-Powell, and the entrepreneurial Sir Donald had made sure the occasion would not be forgotten by offering a challenge cup in his name to be won by the side that excelled most against the English cricketers.

Aubrey's defence of Major Warton was a typical gesture. It also served the purpose of smoothing any ruffled feelings that may have remained from the financial negotiations for the trip. Major Warton, somewhat innocently, had not anticipated that the amateurs' expenses would be more than that required for travel and lodging. He had not allowed for the fact that Aubrey did not have independent means, and therefore a settlement was reached whereby the captain received a quarter more than one of the professionals' salary, which was £100 plus living expenses and a concessionary rate on the railways. Such were the difficulties caused by social distinction, and forced 'shamateurism'. It took two World Wars and a little longer than Aubrey's lifetime to end the charade in cricket.

The short haul to Dartmouth was uneventful, and there Emile McMaster and Maurice Read joined the rest of the side on board, as did £100,000 *in specie*, making in all £300,000 of imperialist gold, silver, nickel and note residing in the Purser's safe. During the short stop-over in Dartmouth, Aubrey and Monty Bowden spent some time scouring the town for 'wigs and other matters theatrical'. Both of them, no doubt, remembering the fun they had had with the amateur dramatics on the boat to Australia the previous year.

The Channel was choppy and the majority succumbed. The Bay of Biscay failed for once to live up to its reputation, and gave the cricketers a chance to bear out Aubrey's words when he had humorously warned Captain Jefferies that he was afraid the side might act like a set of schoolboys and that he would have to excuse any frivolities.

In a letter to the *Evening News* from Lisbon, Aubrey wrote: 'Cricket was started, but without much satisfaction to big hitters, and the team were forced to content themselves with "catch-ball", using apples, turnips and potatoes cribbed from the ship's galley ... We got on shore at Lisbon, where the members of the team wandered about rather hopelessly, not having any Portuguese scholars among them.'

Back on ship the side contented themselves with athletic sports contests, grand concerts and comedies, and in one of these called *Uncles Will* Aubrey took the part of one Charles Cashmore. In the concerts, Major Warton, who in his time had been a church organist, was much in demand as accompanist and solo pianist, and as a gesture to even more colourful entertainment, the tourists agreed to 'black-up' as the *Garth Castle Minstrels*, and the captain (Aubrey, that is) was required to be Mr Boss and sing a mournful ballad called 'Enniscorthy', as well as select a Stump speech.

Eventually the *Garth Castle* steamed into Table Bay, and the flag on Signal Hill announced her arrival. A host of well-wishers clambered aboard with enthusiastic welcomes, and numerous invitations to the Englishmen to attend this and that bazaar, party, function, dinner/dance until it seemed they had to be in three places at the same time. At last they managed to de-ship, with the amateurs putting up at the International Hotel, and the professionals being quartered at the St George's.

According to the press, the welcome the tourists received exceeded anything that had gone before. 'Men of world-wide celebrity, of illustrious rank, of distinguished eminence have come to these shores and have gone without an approach to the commotion that has attended the visit of Major Warton's team.'

No less a personage than His Excellency the Governor, Sir Hercules Robinson, welcomed the new arrivals at the opening reception at Poole's Hotel, and an impressive gathering was made even more so by the presence of the Chief Justice, Sir J. H. de Villiers, flanked by the Speaker of the House of Assembly, Sir David Tennant. Aubrey responded in light-hearted fashion, joking about the matter-of-fact way the locals had reacted to Johnny Briggs' bowling in the nets at Newlands. Did they know what lay in store?

The first match was against Twenty-two of Western Province District, and began on the Friday before Christmas.

The weather was stiflingly hot, and having lost the toss Aubrey led the eleven 'Britishers', who were sporting the chocolate colours of Surrey, together with Union Jack badges and yellow striped ribbons, on to the field to a tremendous roar from an estimated two thousand throats. He opened the bowling with Briggs and took the first three wickets from the Wynberg end. Wickets continued to fall at regular intervals and apart from a typically courageous knock from the Province's captain Milton, there was not much opposition. Because of injury, Bowden took the place of Wood behind the stumps, and deservedly earned a great deal of admiration for his 'keeping, when he had a hand in seven dismissals – five stumped and two caught.

When it came to the Englishmen's turn to bat, they fared little better. A collapse followed a steady opening partnership by Abel and Bowden, and their total of 135, two behind that of the Province, owed a lot to a late flourish from Wood and Roberts. The second innings of both sides almost exactly matched that of their first, only this time the Englishmen finished a little further behind to lose by seventeen runs. At one stage Aubrey looked as if he was going to win the match for the tourists when he dictated the scoring with less than forty runs needed for victory, but the end came quickly after he was bowled by a full toss.

A few weeks later Aubrey wrote an account of the match for *The Sportsman*. He praised the contributions made for Western Province by Milton, Richards, Theunissen and Ashley, commented on Maurice Read's and Fothergill's touch of sunstroke, Bowden's sprained side, his own maimed finger, and continued: 'Our defeat was due in some measure to these casualties, seconded by a series of banquets, etc., but most of all to unexpected prowess in bowling on the part of the Colonials.'

On Christmas Eve the Englishmen were invited to a Smoking Concert at the Exhibition Building, and everyone was expected to do a 'turn'. Aubrey's stentorian bass/baritone was heard to effect in *The Man that struck O'Hara*, and Monty Bowden rendered *Kissing* in a suitably impassioned manner. Part One of the concert had been devoted to a Christy Minstrel entertainment (incredible as that may seem nearly one hundred years later) when most of the team re-enacted their performances from the ship. The half was concluded with an original and laughable episode entitled *Cousin Simmy*. After the interval the Chairman, the Hon. Colonel Schermbrucker, came into his own as he introduced such remarkable items as Mr Smith's Stump Speech – *The Milk in the Cocoanut*, and Captain Baden-Powell's musical sketch *Public Entertainers*. It was nearly Christmas Day when they all rose for 'the Queen'.

The next match started on Boxing Day, and was against a Cape Colony Fifteen, as opposed to twenty-two. All of the side felt hung-over, not only as a result of the festivities, but also because of the news that J. H. Roberts had to return to England immediately as his mother had died. Major Warton regretfully cancelled all immediate public engagements for the players, and also wired home to secure the services of either George Ulyett or J. M. Preston of Yorkshire. In the event, Ulyett was to accept the offer. The tale of woe was accentuated when it was learned that Bowden's side was little better and he would have to have medical attention before being passed fit to play, and that Aubrey was still feeling the effects of the finger injury acquired on the boat. McMaster stepped in for Roberts, and it was perhaps as well that Aubrey won the toss and elected to bat, thereby allowing the side time to assimilate the mishaps in the relative privacy of the pavilion.

After a few overs torrential rain drove the players from the field, but on the resumption Abel, Bowden and Hearne proceeded steadily enough until another collapse saw the side all out for 122. As the match progressed the fifteen took a first innings lead of 37, and in the tourists' second innings it was the middle order's turn to promote a rearguard action. Aubrey top-scored with a sterling 46, and then joined with Briggs and Fothergill in dismissing Cape Colony for 114, twelve runs short of their requirement. It was a morale-boosting victory for the Englishmen, and Aubrey felt pleased to have taken 8 for 75 in the match. Briggs took 12 for 106 overall.

Once more it was a case of 'back to the sea in ships' or rather one ship, as the doughty eleven boarded the *Roslin Castle* for a journey round the southern coast of the continent for Port Elizabeth. On a cool evening before steaming a dance was held under the auspices of Sir Donald Currie (the ship was part of his company's Colonial Mail Line) that was described in the *Cape Times* as 'one of the events of the season'. The ship was decoratively bunted and awned throughout, illuminated by judiciously situated electric light on the hurricane deck, attended by members of the Ministry, Parliament, and officers of the British and Russian men-of-war that were berthed in harbour, and everyone was encouraged into a passably light fantastic mood with an endless supply of military two step and gay lancer provided free of charge by the band of the East Yorkshire Regiment.

If the players had been left in any doubts as to the main purpose of the tour, they were soon dispelled when attending the public luncheon at the Town Hall in Port Elizabeth. There, at the end of the Hall, was the Union Jack supported by two cricket bats, and alongside was a large framed picture of W. G. himself!

The game against twenty-two local stalwarts was played in cloudless conditions on a matting wicket in front of substantial crowds, and resulted in a 55 run win for the home side. The match emphasised the difficulty experienced by practically every South African batsman the tourists were to encounter in playing Briggs, who took 28 wickets for 153 runs, and also high lighted the difficulty of accumulating runs against a field of twenty-two men. It has to be said, though, that exactly half of the English team were dismissed by being clean bowled.

Mossel Bay, the fifth port of the Union, lays claim to the first Post Office and place of worship in South Africa, though certainly it was to its more famous sole and oysters that the team looked forward, as the S.S. *Venice* set out with what seemed to be the whole population of Port Elizabeth waving farewell from the jetty and shore. Unfortunately they were denied the chance to sample the fishy delicacies, as the steamer with the English colours flying from the mast head chugged past Seal Island many hours late, and the players were compelled to set out hurriedly after dark in carts on the long and dangerous trek to Oudtshoorn. Aubrey, who had had to content himself with a modest five wickets in the last match, never forgot that journey:

Only one of the carts which carried us had a light, which was pleasant for us, seeing that the road was very difficult, and that sometimes there were precipices on one side of us.

On the last cart of all were Abel and Fothergill – you may be sure that the one light was not with them. After a time Abel called out in the silence: 'Mr Grieve! Let's hear your voice.' And I can assure you that we were glad enough to hear *his* voice, for it was a very weird ride. Presently the driver of their cart lost his way and got left behind. Fortunately, in the nick of time, we heard Abel shouting out: 'Mr Smith! Don't let us go any further – it's as well to be killed outright as to be frightened to death.' So we stopped and they caught us up. On the next day it rained hard, and we reached Oudtshoorn at dusk in a miserable state, especially as some of the horses broke down on the way. Then we had to cross a river which was swollen so much that there were doubts as to whether it was safe to attempt the passage. However, we all got across except Abel and Fothergill. It was getting very dark, and we began to be anxious about them. It was decided that it was *just* safe for them to cross. It was quite dark when they reached us, and we naturally expected them to be furious. But to our surprise we heard Abel's cheery voice calling out when he landed: 'Mr Smith, this is ripping. I don't care a tuppence for any river in the country.' We found that one of the horsemen on the other side had given him his flask – and we almost wished that we ourselves had been the last to cross, for *we* hadn't been able to get even a sight of a flask for a long time.

Having successfully negotiated the hazards of the swollen Oliphant's River, Aubrey and the team concentrated on the business of outscheming Oudtshoorn, or the South Western Districts XXII as they were variously called. In the event it was not difficult. Oudtshoorn, which is in the Karoo, became the centre of the ostrich farming industry, and their cricketers must have felt like burying their heads in the sand when all twenty-two were out in the first innings for a total of fifty-three. Briggs took 12 for 32, and Aubrey accounted for eight wickets in twenty-three overs and only conceded twelve runs. He also was credited with a stumping off the bowling of the Lancashire man, though in fact the correct reading should be run out. Aubrey then hit a sparkling fifty in the English innings of 268, and took a further six wickets for twenty-three in Oudtshoorn's second knock. It all added up to a convincing win by an innings and eighty runs.

As the tour progressed each group of organisers and reception committees tried to outdo their predecessors in the way of balls, banquets and 'things to do'. Kimberley was no exception, but there, of course, they had the advantage of the diamond mines. So along with a Grand Promenade Concert (cancelled at the last moment) and Pyrotechnic Display, Pirates Bands, smoking concerts (where Aubrey rattled off his two Irish ditties to great applause), dinners, luncheons, parties, etc. etc., there was inevitably a cave visit, which started at the unearthly hour of five in the morning! The town was *en fête* and the two cricket matches in the week became almost an afterthought.

'Well! Well!' said Johnny Briggs, as the team entered the ground. 'Have we got to play cricket on that?' 'That' was a brick red, grassless stretch of land, patched with sprinklings of white sand swept in by the wind, and an asphalt hard surface. It was small wonder that in the trying heat, with their mouths like lime-kilns and their tongues like hearthrugs (Aubrey's own phrase), and with the odds stacked against them by way of numbers, the tourists lost both games. For the Kimberley District XVIII Aubrey's fellow old Carthusian, C. H. Vintcent, excelled, making 87, which was the highest score for either side in any of the tour matches thus far, and playing a part in many of the dismissals. Aubrey did have the satisfaction of bowling him for a duck in his second innings, when Kimberley lost seven wickets before making the thirty-four they needed for victory. It was at this penultimate point in the game that the Kimberley camp felt a few tremors, as Aubrey sent back 4 for 9. The tremors were not felt at the gate, where the 'take' was well over £1,000 for the match. Against the Cape Colony XV the receipts were even better, though the form of the exhausted tourists was not, and they were defeated by ten wickets.

In his speech at the post-match prandials, Aubrey stated that he felt cricket to be the rottenest of games. (No, no.) 'Yes it is, to come 6,000 miles only to make 5 runs in 4 innings – I don't know of a more rotten game. (Loud laughter). We have come as a team to Kimberley, and we have been defeated. We can receive our defeat, because we are Englishmen, and every Englishman knows how to accept defeat, but as Englishmen, while admitting we have been beaten, we will repeat, as the cricket poet did after the defeat of Surrey by the Australians, "Wait till they come back again." ' (Loud laughter and cheers.)

Every tour, short or long, is a roller-coaster of 'ups and downs', the results tending to reflect the side's mental state and appetite for the game. There is always a depressed point, and it had been reached by the Englishmen. They were still not half way through the trip; it had taken a long time to acclimatise; and there seemed to be no end to the incessant round of travel, cricket and hospitality. Their appetite was sated, their sleep was short, and their morale was low. Not that they were ungrateful for the enormous trouble their hosts had taken to make them welcome. It was just that sheer tiredness had taken its toll, and second wind was some time in coming. The South Africans had bowled more penetratively than anticipated; Ulyett, who was replacing Roberts, had not yet arrived; and with Skinner a virtual passenger (he scored one run and took one catch on the entire trip), it meant that Aubrey had very little difficulty in deciding who should play.

A coach took the weary band to the new capital of the South African gold fields, Johannesburg. The Wanderers Club had undertaken major excavation and levelling of the pitch in order to make it ready for the great day, and a crowd of three thousand assembled to see their twenty-two heroes commence battle.

Half way through the encounter it seemed their sights were set straight for victory as, with the exception of Briggs, the English eleven had offered only token resistance. Johannesburg had made 138 in their visit to the crease, and the tourists' response to the bowling of Cooley and Wishart was a miserly sixty. Then the game altered dramatically. C. A. S. and J. B. tore the Jo'burg second innings asunder, and they were forced to retreat in lame disorder for fifty-eight. Johnny Briggs took 9 for 19, and Aubrey 10 for 23, with eight of his victims clean bowled. It was left to Abel and Hearne to make the required 137, which they did without losing their wickets.

The Englishmen's fortunes had changed with their spirits – the line on the graph was now pointing upwards, and so was the gold market on 'Change. A few shrewd and well-advised investments had enabled the team to capitalise, and this was a decisive factor in tempting Aubrey, Monty Bowden, Basil Grieve and Charlie Coventry to stay in South Africa when the tour was completed. Speculation was rife; hourly there were reports of further gold mines; would-be prospectors in town raised excitement to fever pitch; but at the moment, though, for the team it was back to the business in hand.

Both a Transvaal XV and Pietermaritzburg Districts XXII were dispatched with an innings to spare, and against the boys from the capital city of Natal, Aubrey took eleven wickets, which he said was by way of celebrating the belated arrival of George Ulyett. A Natal XI succumbed without the tourists needing to bat a second time, and it was left to a Durban Districts XVIII to stem the avalanche of victories by an innings.

After three days the game resulted in a closely contested draw, the first of the tour, with the Districts being twenty-nine short and having three wickets in hand. Aubrey took ten in the match, and for a while afterwards seemed to be constantly on his feet making impromptu speeches in response to enthusiastic cheers, first on the verandah of the pavilion and then in the Mayor's Parlour. The format of these speeches around the Union seldom altered, a gracious thanking of the hosts, mention of the game and the noteworthy performances, a few humorous quips, and a sentimental summation extolling the spirit of comradeship and goodwill between the Old Country and the Colonies. All highly innocuous wordplay in the best traditions of the Diplomatic Corps, yet obviously expected and always well received. Aubrey, expert in its delivery, made himself extremely popular with everybody. And just in case there were a few still slightly sceptical about the sincerity of the speech, Aubrey had a winning habit of 'improvising' verses to his song, *Ballyhoolly:*

> Before I close my song,
> I think 'twould not be wrong,
> To thank you for your kindly hospitality;
> On our visit to Natal
> I'm sure that we all shall

Look back with more than open partiality.
For our worthy friend, the Mayor,
With most paternal care,
Saw that in Durban's heat we lived right coolly;
For he dosed our aching heads
With his own particular meds,
Faith, they always call it fizz in Ballyhoolly.
  (Tumultuous applause)

A newspaper columnist at the time commented wryly that 'Mr Smith is a fine fellow, a good companion, and an awful favourite with the ladies.'

The departure from Durban was spectacular. Early on the Sunday morning three tramloads of supporters accompanied the team to the Point, where they were to board Sir Donald's *Drummond Castle* for the trip to East London. Nearly all the vessels in harbour were proudly displaying bunting in honour of the visitors, and there was a cacophony of shouting, hooting and cheering. Getting aboard the *Drummond Castle* provided a first-class circus turn, as a tug, the *Fox*, had to transfer the cricketers through the shallower waters from shore to ship. This left a choice of rope ladder or basket as a means of getting aboard, and Major Warton, who was among the first to venture on to the ladder, nearly fell back into the tug and lost his hat to the sea in the attempt. Then Bobby Abel, who never could find his 'sea-legs', tried to scale the ladder about a dozen times to the accompaniment of uncontrollable laughter and unhelpful advice from those below, before finally admitting defeat and accepting the comparative safety of the hoisted basket. Maurice Read and George Ulyett thought that that was a good idea too, and by the time the steamer pulled anchor and set off it was practically noon.

From East London to King Williamstown was a short haul, and there at the Victoria Recreation Grounds were twenty-two Cape Mounted Riflemen, soon to be shot to smithereens in two successive matches. In the first match Briggs did the damage, and in the second Aubrey captured nineteen wickets for sixty-six runs, hitting the stumps directly on fourteen occasions.

A Grahamstown XXII provided further easy meat on the

'City Lord's', an attractive ground with a view of the hills surrounding the cathedral city, and it was another victory with an innings to spare with Aubrey helping himself to fifteen at an average of nearly four runs per wicket.

The team then decamped for an engagement against a Midland Districts XXII on the Recreation Ground at Graaff-Reinet, which was so called in 1786 after the Governor of the Cape, General von der Graaff and his wife. Graaff-Reinet was the scene of the short-lived Boer Republic in 1795, and became a substantial agricultural region dealing in cattle, flowers, fruit and ostrich feathers. The Gem team submitted gracefully on the 'brak' ground, similar to that at Kimberley, and the Englishmen did not have to pad up a second time. At the customary close of play banquet, both Major Warton and Aubrey declared their thanks for a reception which they said had not been surpassed by any town they had visited on the tour. After what had gone before, it takes some believing!

The tourists now were on the home run, and returned to Port Elizabeth to beat an Eastern Province XV by eight wickets, with Fothergill acting as chief destroyer on a dyed green matting strip. Then came the first of the two most important matches on the tour – a game against a South African XI, which was subsequently given Test status and became, therefore, the first Test Match between the two countries. In spite of high expectations in the Colony, the South Africans were beaten convincingly by eight wickets, and were never really in the game with a chance after being dismissed for eighty-four in their first innings. Aubrey mopped up the 'tail' in his 5 for 19, but, more importantly, took the vital wicket of A. B. Tancred, the Kimberley opener. After the match there were the usual presentations of gold medals, diamond tie-pins and liberally filled purses. As the fixture had finished early, it was decided to hold a scratch match between Married and Single Players in order to entertain the many visitors to the town; however, it finished inconclusively.

Aubrey now went down with a fever. Several of the side had been afflicted similarly during the tour, and it was not surprising considering the insanitary conditions prevalent. He was too ill to travel to Kimberley, and Bowden acted as skipper in his place. The match against an Eighteen ended with the visitors getting the better of a draw, and Johnny Briggs making ninety-three not out.

Aubrey had just recovered in time for the final match, the Second Test against a South African XI at Capetown, but unfortunately he was unable to make the journey from Kimberley before play was scheduled to start. The team managed very well without him, as they devastated the Colonials with an innings and 202 runs to spare. With time in hand, another match was started which gave the South Africans a chance to save face by providing more respectable opposition, and it concluded with their score at 123 for 6 in reply to Major Warton's team's 248.

After the farewell luncheon, dinner, presentations and speeches, where it was unanimously agreed that the tour had been highly successful from all points of view (not least statistically: Aubrey had accumulated 134 wickets, and Johnny Briggs more than twice that), Aubrey and Monty Bowden waved goodbye to Major Warton and the team from the steam yacht *Dalcon* as it sailed alongside of the *Garth Castle* after it had left the harbour. They were feeling a little fragile as an average of two bottles of wine per man had been drunk at the goodbye gathering on the boat the night before. They also were feeling sad and just a touch apprehensive about their future as the yacht finally relinquished its rôle as escort and turned back to port, where the huge crowd who had gathered to cheer the team off still mingled, reluctant to depart and admit their feelings of anti-climax.

For young men in their mid-twenties it was an adventurous step to leave their homeland, permanently as they then thought, and take a chance on stockbroking. Monty Bowden had the advantage of several years of experience gained as an exchange clerk in London, whereas Aubrey had barely touched the fringes as an assistant to a friend of the family. The good-looking Bowden was the more impetuous of the two, and tended on occasions to give himself 'airs' which could be irritating. Nevertheless, the tour had cemented a friendship which seemed to be the attraction of opposites. Aubrey by nature was more cautious, though he liked a gamble, reliable and far from superficial.

After a short rest to recover from the exertions of the tour, both Aubrey and Monty went about setting up business. They joined the ranks of Randt shareholders, as did Basil Grieve and a brother-in-law of the Queen's daughter, Lord Walter Campbell; then they formed their own partnership, Smith and Bowden, on the Johannesburg Stock Exchange, and in a very short time they began to prosper. Grieve also started as a broker, and waited for the promised return of Major Warton to keep him company; the Hon. Charles Coventry decided to join the Bechuanaland Police.

Even in 1889, with duckboards in use as pavements, it was difficult to visualise Johannesburg as Ferreira's Camp of three years earlier when gold was discovered. The town and population were expanding daily, alive to the sound of nuggets, and into this galvanic activity the partners flung themselves with confident enthusiasm. Naturally, amongst the work there was a modicum of play.

'Mr Smith's versatile talents enable him to play many parts in the world's stage and to shine in all.' Aubrey had availed himself of the opportunity to relax with the part of Captain Hawksley in *Still Waters Run Deep*, which J. A. Rosier was putting on at the Theatre Royal. The rôle was doubly attractive, as Aubrey remembered most of the lines from his performances at Cambridge, and therefore less preparation was needed. Were there any premonitions of the future as the villainous Captain Hawksley plotted with a financier in the City? 'His histrionic powers, though not equal to his cricket, are by no means deserving of adverse criticism and altogether he may be congratulated on having made a very passable first appearance.'

After commenting on the character played by J. A. Rosier, the critic went on: 'Mr Smith's athletic figure, too, in comparison with Mr Rosier's more delicate one, unsuits them in this particular for their respective parts, as it is rather an anomaly to see Mr Rosier overcome Mr Smith by physical force, and to hear the former vaunt his superior bodily vigour.'

During the next year Aubrey took part in a number of these semi-amateur theatricals as they were described. 'One of his greatest successes' was the verdict for Captain Blake in *The Scrap of Paper*; 'effectively aristocratic and oratically perfect' was the decision in favour of Sir Geoffrey Champneys in *Our*

Boys; Lionel Leveret in *Old Soldiers* (another old rôle) was performed with 'style and finish, and an absolute freeness from the tricks and manners of the amateur'; and Offenbach's *Two Blind Beggars* was 'impersonated by "two stoneybrokers" (another hint) presumably Messrs C. A. Smith and C. H. Cause'.

Then there were the smoking concerts, where lovers of nicotine and notes showed off their latest *à la mode* pipeware. Unfortunately, on one occasion the ladies were present, and it 'seemed to deter the major portion of the gentlemen from enjoying the weed.' There were compensations. 'Aubrey gave a capital imitation of an Irish nigger, with a brogue thick enough to cut.'

His other speciality at these evenings was a heart-rending performance of *Recollections of a Duck*. Enough said.

Nor did Aubrey neglect the sporting life. He was elected captain of the Wanderers football team, and led them in the final of the Transvaal Association Challenge Cup against Wasps. On a hard sandy surface, even with the lightest of boots, it was difficult to keep up with the leather, and yet 'Smith repeatedly drew forth cheers for his splendid footwork, and twice within a few minutes he had passed the ball on to Britten, after carrying it down the right wing, both times a goal being the result.' Wanderers won the game 3-2.

At cricket, again Aubrey captained the Wanderers. Pretoria were dismissed for twenty-two, and he claimed seven victims. Surprisingly at the concert after the match Aubrey sang *Oh, what a happy land is England*. He grabbed a further six for the Stock Exchange against the World, when he 'shared' the bowling with Abe Bailey, who was to become such a potent force in South African cricket, and was also scheduled to turn out for the Mother Country versus the Colonial Born. There was then a theatrical contest, and also Fancy Dress cricket with one side dressed in all white and the other completely in black. Aubrey played as the mocking Mephistopheles!

The final absurdity for those who treated the game as nothing short of religion was when a Professor Cogan, who claimed to be the South African Blondin, conducted a 'cricket match' from the high wire, with four of the Wanderers at the Club ground. Two poles were placed a pitch-length apart and suspended between them was a slack wire on which the

Professor stood. The wicket was suspended from one end of the wire. The opposition consisted of Monty Bowden, Alsopp, Mosenthal and Aubrey, and the incredible 'Prof' managed to score sixty-nine runs before he was bowled. He, in turn, then bowled from the wire against the four who, needless to say, were at ground level, and got them all out for 113, though they were handicapped by having to use a pick-handle instead of a bat. Aubrey made most of the runs, though he was considered fortunate after he had been bowled first ball with the trial delivery.

While all this high jinking had been going on, the firm of Smith and Bowden had been doing very nicely, thank you, but in such an intoxicated situation with office clerks, drapery assistants and even churchmen dabbling in shares and keeping the market in a continual state of ferment, the inevitable finally happened. Aubrey recalled the time in an interview for the *Cricket Field* in May of 1895: 'When the boom burst lots of men had overdrafts of £50,000 or so and the bank, of course, wanted the money. Nevertheless we did very well, and if we had continued we might have met with considerable success. But months of intense heat were followed by a time of famine, and we both got ill.'

And Aubrey became so ill that he was near the not so golden gate. He had contracted the common typhoid fever caused by the contaminated water supply, and also a dose of pleurisy and pneumonia to boot! When the fever was at its height he began hallucinating, and reliving a kaleidoscope of recent experience: the courtyard was very large and steep, and he began to feel it moving up and down. 'I've drunk too much, I must have.' He looked again. The courtyard was still moving up and down. 'I don't feel too good.' All of a sudden everything was enveloped in shadow. A horde of flying ants took off! – He was in an ox wagon, and there at the side of the track – 'Don't move!' shouted the rancher. 'Don't move – wait till they've crossed!' The old baboon stood at the top of the mound with malevolent stare, as the young troop frolicked across their path in an untidy heap. 'It's unsafe to get in their way.' The troop were across, and slowly the old baboon lumbered in their wake—

DEATH OF MR AUBREY SMITH

Information has been received that Mr Aubrey Smith, who captained the English team during the Cricket Tournament, has succumbed to that fell disease, inflammation of the lungs. For some time past he was confined to his room; but as he took a turn for the better it was thought that he had successfully tided over the crisis. Much regret will be felt at his decease, as during his tour through the Colony and his short stay at the Rand he made many friends by his kindly disposition.

The *Graaff-Reinet Advertiser's* obituary was fifty-nine years, two months and three days premature.

Eventually Aubrey was found in a very weakened state, semi-conscious, not having eaten properly for weeks, with only a bottle of Van der Humm and a large but nearly empty tin of Huntley and Palmer's biscuits for company. Friends were called. Mrs Fricker and Arthur Marshall nursed him back to health.

At the time of the pronouncement of his death, an official from the Wanderers Club came to his lodgings to enquire whether the club band might officiate at the funeral! Apparently the cadaver was vastly amused.

A week or so after he had 'died' Aubrey went to recuperate at a quiet farm near Krugersdorp, which apparently was close to a crocodile river. As Anna, Comtesse de Bremont (who had Gaelic ancestry and came from Cincinnati, Ohio) informed her readers in her local column, the farm was 'far from the madding crowd, but not far enough to escape the visits of the "boys" who find Krugersdorp, given a fine day minus the dust, a delightful spin out of camp.'

Aubrey gradually recovered his equilibrium, and found his way back to the cricket field. He was convinced that there was enough cricketing strength in Johannesburg to warrant the Transvaal challenging Kimberley for the Currie Cup which had been presented to them for the best performances against Major Warton's side. He also relished a chance to turn the tables against the Griquas, and so in due course, having gathered general agreement for the idea, a match was arranged.

Charlie Vintcent, C. E. Finlason, Monty Bowden and, of

course, Aubrey formed the nucleus of the Transvaal side, and
A. B. Tancred, the 'W. G. of South Africa', and A. R. Innes
were expected to be the champions for Kimberley. Prior to the
game, which became historically significant as the first recognised Currie Cup Tournament, Aubrey had organised trial
fixtures to test individual form, and give much needed practice
to the team.

The match lacked nothing in excitement. Kimberley batted
first and were bowled out for ninety-eight, with Bentley
Wimble and Aubrey taking four apiece, and Tancred scoring
forty-two. Then Transvaal struggled to get 117, with Bowden
contributing sixty-three, and in Kimberley's second knock
Tancred made a century, which left Transvaal needing a total
in excess of two hundred in order to win. This they managed
easily through a magnificent not out century from Bowden, and
a sterling job as night watchman from Aubrey. Amid the
scenes of jubilation Aubrey felt, though he wisely kept his
feelings to himself, that at last he had honoured his promise 'to
come back again'.

On 'Change there was no jubilation. The crash with its
Black Tuesdays, and even blacker Fridays had scuttled many a
heady financier, and the firm of Smith and Bowden had
suffered along with the rest. Aubrey had decided to return to
England and take up a so-called 'lucrative offer' on the London
Stock Exchange, when he became aware of a speculation that
Monty Bowden had arranged that left the firm owing over
£1,300 to H. F. Mosenthal, who was a fellow member of the
Wanderers, brother cricketer and born actor.

Bowden had disappeared, gone 'up-country' some thought,
and Aubrey was left with no option but to raise as much cash as
he could himself to repay the debt. He managed to find £1,000
and promised more when he could scrape it together. Mosenthal, who had played Podger and Major Fang in *Old Soldiers* and
whose stage presence in *Our Bitterest Foe* was described as
'masculine, manly, magnificent and martial', agreed, and
eventually on receipt of a further £100 waived the remainder of
the debt.

The transaction left Aubrey virtually penniless. Fortunately,
the colourful Barnatos, Barney and Harry, with a love of
theatre nurtured in the music-halls of Whitechapel, gave him

crucial assistance, and he still had retained his return boat ticket for home.

The Wanderers Club organised a farewell dinner and concert in his honour, and it turned out to be a nostalgic evening, full of *bonhomie* and bathos. The Bowden affair had been successfully 'hushed-up', and he was next heard of as one of Cecil Rhodes' Pioneers. Later he became a liquor-runner, before one day at the start of the rainy season, when he was probably weak and light-headed from fever and whisky, he fell from his wagon and died under the feet of his oxen.

In years to come Aubrey always looked back to his time in South Africa with a rosy glow, yet as the *Grantully Castle* steamed past Robben Island with the Cape receding into the distance, and as he leaned on the deck rail clutching a fistful of affectionate good luck and 'bon voyage' telegrams, no doubt he would have liked to have met the journalist who had sometime christened Johannesburg 'the city of the second chance'.

Who would have guessed this was a perfect English gentleman? (Honor Cobb collection)

The Charterhouse Fire Brigade. Aubrey is on extreme right, back row. (Courtesy of Dr Fernandez-Armisto, Charterhouse Library)

T. Sandford.
A.H. Sharman.
F.W. Betterill.
H.S. Gill
C.A. Smith (Captain)
E. Fisher
H. Ward
T.W. Peck
G.A. Messop.

Captain of St John's College Football XI, minus two. (Courtesy of N. C. Buck, Libraria
St John's College, Cambridge)

F. Thomas
Phillips
F.H. Gresson
Humphreys
Tate
C.A. Smith
Hide T.
Hide A.
G. Brann
Quaife
W. Newham

A determined and enthusiastic skipper of the struggling Sussex County side. (Roger Man
collection)

...ene from J. M. Barrie's *Alice Sit By The Fire* at the Duke of York's Theatre, 1905. Dora Hole is the ...e and Ellen Terry Mrs Grey. (Courtesy of the Theatre Department, Victoria and Albert Museum)

For those in peril on the sea: Aubrey rescues Florence Deshon in *Jafferay*, a silent picture directed by George Irving at Atlantic City in 1915. (Honor Cobb collection)

Aubrey's colour sketch of the view from Westminster Bridge when on Night Duty with the Artist during the First World War. (Honor Cobb collection)

The commemorative shield that decorated Hollywood Cricket Club's pavilion at Griffith Park. (Hollywood Cricket Club collection)

'e Round Corner' at the top of Coldwater Canyon with stumps and bat on the roof of the garage.
(Honor Cobb collection)

ing delivery during net practice from the Grand Old Man, aged 73. (Courtesy of National Film
Archive/Stills Library)

Hollywood Cricket Club visited Vancouver during the summer of 1936. This team photo includes
Lawton (middle row, third from right); Errol Flynn and Nigel Bruce (left of front row); and To▸
Freebairn-Smith and Claude King (right of front row). (Thomas Freebairn-Smith collectio▸

A study in concentration,
Vancouver 1936. (Thomas
Freebairn-Smith collection)

C team stops off in Hollywood on its return from the Australian tour of 1936/37, and watches the
of the David O. Selznick production of *The Prisoner of Zenda*. Front row: Aubrey, Bruce Harris of
ening Standard, Bill Voce, tour manager Rupert Howard, Ken Farnes; and in the background:
Barnett, Hedley Verity, Laurie Fishlock, Wally Hammond and Jim Sims. (Courtesy of Russell
Birdwell, Selznick International Pictures)

fixed the drinks? Aubrey as Colonel Zapt with David Niven as Fritz von Tarlenheim and an
Ronald Colman (Rudolf Rassendyll/the King) in *The Prisoner of Zenda*. (David Niven collection)

More than sixty years on. Aubrey takes a last look at his old study at St John's College, Cambridge 1947, the year before he died. (Honor Cobb collection)

5/From Amateur to Professional

My prediction of last week that Mr C. A. Smith would, in all probability, reach England at the end of this month has turned out to be accurate. I was unfortunate enough to miss 'Round the Corner' myself when he paid me a flying visit at my official residence on Tuesday morning on his way through London to Brighton. I gather, however, from those who did see him that he was in the best of health and spirits. His exuberance at seeing a real cricket ground again after a long spell of the artificial substitute can easily be imagined. That he was eager to get to work again was shown by the fact that he had hardly reached Brighton before he was away to the County ground to open his shoulders with a little practice. His many friends will be heartily pleased to hear of his safe return to the old country.

The editor, C. W. Alcock, writing in the magazine *Cricket*.

Sussex cricket was in the doldrums. The previous season when Aubrey was in South Africa they had again finished bottom of the County table. Their supporters were crying out for new recruits. Humphreys, they said, was past it, Newham was distracted by the cares of captaincy and, apart from the Hide brothers, and maybe Bean and Quaife, the rest were no good. There were great hopes that Aubrey's return as captain would make all the difference.

The Sussex trial match at the beginning of May, when he played for the Club and Ground, augured well for his own form. On a soft pitch against seventeen Colts he took fifteen wickets and three catches. Again at Lord's, in the annual opening skirmish with M.C.C. and Ground, he devastated the opposition in their second innings with 7 for 16 from twelve overs, which virtually ensured a Sussex victory, and among the sacrificial lambs were a few 'old mutton' such as Hornby, Flowers, Attewell and Sherwin. But after that, with the season barely under way, there was just *one* further victory.

A colossal away defeat by Notts, in which C. A. S. was deficited with 130 runs after sixty-one overs with but a solitary wicket to show, was followed by the single ray of sunshine when Gloucestershire were convincingly conquered by 221 runs, due mainly to the magnificent batting of Quaife. Aubrey had the distinction of being adjudged l.b.w. to W. G. Grace for thirty-three, as well as acquiring 4 for 70. The remainder of the season was unrelieved disaster, with nearly every defeat being by an innings. *Wisden* recorded that 'C. A. Smith worked all through the summer with an amount of energy that deserved a far better reward. He at least never lost heart and played in match after match with as much determination as though he had the good fortune to be on the winning side.' There was the occasional personal satisfaction to savour, often with his improved batting: a forty against Yorkshire at Bradford, forty-six and fifty-eight not out in two appearances against the touring Australians, a top score of sixty-one against Hampshire. But then again, there were far too many unsatisfactory and unhappy memories, particularly when Cambridge came to Brighton in June. After a moderate first knock when Aubrey had dismissed 5 for 57, Cambridge amassed a gigantic 703 for 9 declared, with F. G. J. Ford, C. P. Foley and G. McGregor all scoring hundreds. This was practically the only time in Aubrey's career when his bowling proved expensive. As he led his demoralised troops into the pavilion, four of the bowlers had 'centuries' against their names, and his own debit was 1 for 117 after thirty overs.

After such a catastrophic run of defeat, it was no surprise when the Sussex Committee voted to bring back Newham as captain for the next season. They had not forgotten that he had led the side with a fair measure of success when Aubrey was in South Africa. A change of leader might alter the side's fortunes; it was not possible for things to get worse.

That winter Aubrey pursued his interest in semi-professional dramatics, stage managing 'one-nighters' at country houses, helping at the Brighton Green Room Club where his sister Beryl 'starred' quite frequently under the stage name of Beryl Faber, and appearing in such familiar rôles as Charles Cashmore in *Uncles Will* for the Preston Hypocrites. A production of *Two Roses*, a comedy by James Albery, saw him on stage with both his sisters, Beryl and Myrtle, and in the following April he acted in a benefit for an orphan boys' home in the Clarence Rooms at the Hotel Metropole, Brighton.

The production was *A Sheep in Wolf's Clothing*, a play by Tom Taylor, and 'Mr C. A. Smith, looking lordly and large, did capitally as Jasper Carew, although occasionally he seemed to think all this rare good fun rather than a serious revelation of the soul of a "human man" of the Cavalier time.' And lo and behold, 'looking awfully nice as Colonel Kirk in that lovely red and white costume' was none other than the lone creditor from the distant Cape, H. F. Mosenthal, no doubt hot foot after the loot. He also joined Aubrey in a curtain-raiser called *In Honour Bound*, which, considering the circumstances of two of his performers, was a little tactless of the playwright, Mr Grundy. The programme printers did their best to help with 'honour' spelt 'honor'.

As David Kynaston's excellent article in a recent *Wisden Cricket Monthly* reveals, in June 1891 Aubrey met the committee of the London Stock Exchange. The 'lucrative offer' of just over a year ago had been impossible to pursue while money was still owed on behalf of the firm Smith and Bowden, and he had had to content himself by working on the fringes of the Exchange as a half-commissioned man, bringing business to a member for execution. The rest of his time when not playing cricket or acting was spent doing spots of teaching when and where he could.

Now, having given Mosenthal a further £100, and with a receipt for full discharge of all claims in his hand, Aubrey was hoping to gain admission to the Exchange. Mr W. Lindo had filed an application for Aubrey to become his unauthorised clerk, and the Committee listened attentively while the sordid saga of Johannesburg was related to them. The Committee minutes reveal then that Rule 30 was read, 'after which it was moved by Mr Keen, seconded by Mr Costello, that a Committee be specially convened under Rule 19 to consider the question of dispensing with the strict enforcement of Rule

30' in this particular case. 'Upon a division, 8 voted for and 8 against the motion, which was accordingly declared not to be carried—' Rule 30 presumably was a clause prohibiting admission to those who had not refunded in full any debt, and Rule 19 probably allowed further consideration for what were thought to be special cases. Thank goodness Aubrey was not compelled to spend the rest of his life incarcerated with the 'bulls and bears' of the trading floor. What would the stage and screen have lost!

Meanwhile Sussex were having their best season for a long time, and in all matches finished with as many won as lost. Aubrey took four in each innings against Notts at Trent Bridge, and turned in several useful batting performances, highlighted by undefeated fifties against Kent and Middlesex. *Wisden* announced 'Mr C. A. Smith had a notable share in the success, playing an invaluable first innings of 50 not out and taking in the second innings of Middlesex five wickets for only 25 runs.' Stoddart was one of the victims, and Aubrey conceded the runs from nineteen overs, which can be interpreted as economical yet assertive bowling. The summary of his summer's labour was condensed with 'Mr Smith, it will be seen, comes out with a capital record in all the average tables, being third in batting and first in bowling in first class county engagements, and sixth in batting and third in bowling in all matches.'

In later years Aubrey always gave 1892 as the year in which he ceased to be involved with the first class game, though in fact he played more games for Sussex in the two following seasons. Naturally his thinking had been conditioned by his first full professional engagement on the boards in the August of that year. It was a watershed in his life, the end of one existence, the start of another; for him at that time acting had usurped cricket in importance.

It had not exactly been a winter of discontent, though Aubrey was far from satisfied with the way things were going. The future was uncertain, schoolmastering or broking he had now decided were not for him in the long term, cricket for Sussex without the captaincy was not quite as attractive, and in any case it was a seasonal activity and there could not be many more years ahead; acting, which seemed to be taking up more and more of his time, he enjoyed immensely, though amateur and semi-professional engagements did not provide a living. The uncertainty was reflected in the nine matches that he did play for the County.

'Mr C. A. Smith was not able to play so often as in the previous year and no doubt suffered from the want of regular practice. His bowling was altogether ineffective and in batting he was also less successful than before,' concluded *Wisden* in the following year.

There were three or four 'knocks' worth remembering. He always had done well at the expense of Hampshire, and even in this desultory summer for Aubrey, they suffered. At Brighton in June he cracked fifty in the first innings and seventy-nine in the second, and when Notts visited a month later he helped himself to forty-nine and forty-one. He twice fell victim to W. G. Grace's wiles, and this could be said to be an amicable family revenge for Aubrey's many previous dismissals of his brother E. M. Throughout the season Aubrey only trundled 101 overs for Sussex, and in company with the other bowlers saw many a potential victim dropped either at the wicket or in the field.

In May of that year the dramatic critic of the *Daily Telegraph* had attended a performance at the Brighton Green Room Club and mentioned C. A. Smith as 'an actor who might well, if he desired to do so, turn his attention to the stage,' (dropping a seed in his mind) … 'He is tall, good-looking, and with a winning and natural manner that contrasts well with the staginess and stilted fashion of many of our modern young men. Mr C. A. Smith has in him all the elements of a good actor. He only wants "extending", as racing men say. He began better than he ended, for the simple reason that where he wanted help, that assistance was denied him.'

The *Cricket Field*, which reproduced this notice in the issue for the 21st May 1892, added: 'After these flattering criticisms "Round the Corner Smith" … may almost be pardoned for a slight show of vanity. There is this time no mistake about his identity, as was the case a few months ago when he was embarrassed by receiving congratulations upon inheriting a fortune, which had been left to another C. A. Smith also of Brighton.'

How Aubrey must have wished there had been no mistake! Apart from the above, there was another Smith with virtually the same initials running theatrical enterprises in Brighton for a time, which caused considerable confusion, and when he was at Cambridge, Aubrey remembered hearing of 'Gentleman Smith, the Actor', who had attended St John's after leaving Eton and played three matches at cricket against All England. In the England side there were also two Smiths, one of them Captain Smith of Sussex. For a time the surname Smith seemed to guarantee captaincy of the County. In just over thirty years there were three of that name who led the side on to the cricket field – C. H., C. A. and C. L. A.

When appearing at the Brighton Green Room Club Aubrey had several times been stage managed by A. B. Tapping, who, with his partner Cartwright, had a professional company that undertook long provincial tours. That August Tapping was frantically searching for a replacement in the company, as illness had struck even the assigned understudies, and so he contacted an actor/manager who he thought might be able to help, Ben Greet. Greet was a kind of catalyst for newcomers to the stage, and yet every actor he suggested seemed to be already working or away on holiday. In the course of conversation Greet mentioned Aubrey whom he had seen recently, and Tapping, who had been impressed by C. A.'s portrayals of Douglas Cattermole in *The Private Secretary* and Jack Wyatt in *Two Roses*, accepted the thought with alacrity. Several times before, he had suggested to Aubrey that he might consider joining his company, and each time the matter had been left unresolved. Now, however, Aubrey was in a quandary about his future, needed a job, and so it was that he came to make a professional début in repertory at Hastings.

It had not been an easy decision to make. Even though he loved the theatre, in those days for someone of his background and social position to go on stage for money was regarded as 'not quite the thing'. His mother had cried: 'Aubrey, Aubrey, don't go on the stage, think of what will become of your two sisters if their brother is an actor', and the counsel given by a number of friends was *réculer pour mieux sauter*; because for them acting was rather raffish. In fact, unbelievably, in the 1970s there were still a few diehards who thought the same.

The well-known actor/author and after-dinner speaker Dennis Castle remembers standing in the players' tearoom in the Hove Pavilion where there hangs a portrait of Aubrey in his later years. Castle was admiring the nobility of the hawk-like nose, the gentleness in the deep eyes, when an ancient Sussex member standing at his elbow voiced his thoughts. 'Good all-rounder, played for England, soccer for the Corinthians but ... well ... it was such a drawback his being a mummer by profession ...'

'Look after the consonants, my boy,' impressed Greet, 'and the vowels will look after themselves.' Aubrey never forgot this advice as he took to the stage playing three different parts in *Jim the Penman* on two separate tours; taking the rôle of the American and also the lead in *The Idler*; and making an appearance in *Not such a fool as he looks*.

After this I joined the 'Bootle's Baby' touring company, and took the title rôle (not the Baby). I had one positively awful experience when we were playing at Nottingham during the match between Notts and Gloucestershire. I was in the middle of a love scene with the heroine when, to my horror, a long file of cricketers, headed by W. G., trooped slowly into the stalls. It was an experience I shall never forget. In the play mention was made of an officer who had several children, and the cricketers took this up with great glee, and I never could convince them that I wasn't putting in some gag for the benefit of E. M. After the piece was over W. G. came behind, and was very nice and kind.

Following this episode, there must have been even greater laughter a week later when E. M. caught Aubrey in both innings in the match between Sussex and Gloucestershire at Bristol in the early August of '93. Aubrey was not left entirely pointless, however, as he had made twenty-seven in his second visit to the crease, and also dismissed younger brother W. G. Earlier in the season he had taken seventy off the Gloucestershire attack when they came to Brighton. *Wisden* reports that 'the only batting worthy of special mention was that shown by C. A. Smith and W. Newham, who between them scored 104 runs out of 192 obtained from the bat. There was a marked contrast in their styles. Newham played with extreme caution, while Smith hit with great brilliancy. In fourth wicket down at seventy-five, Smith was ninth out at 194, the chief hits in his admirable though not faultless innings being twelve 4's, a 3 and five 2's.' Our old friend Albert Craig had been in attendance. He had been more impressed by Aubrey's bowling:

> Hurrahs for the friends of the ball and the bat,
> To Mr Smith's bowling I take off my hat.
> Old Sussex beat Glo'ster, how pleasant it sounds,
> You'll soon see them rising by leaps and by bounds.

The prediction was not entirely accurate, because at the final count Sussex had sedately stepped up two places to seventh.

During the summer Aubrey also culled thirty-five from Notts and fifty-three from Somerset; batting had assumed a much greater importance in his cricket. The next season too saw a consistent though moderate level of scoring, with the match against Middlesex, in which he accumulated a total of seventy-seven runs and four wickets, being the best overall performance. And so far as first class cricket went, that was it. Apart from a solitary appearance against Hampshire at Southampton in 1896, Aubrey rested on his laurels. Laurels which were now being won slowly on the stage with an invitation to join John Hare and Mrs Patrick Campbell at London's Garrick Theatre for *The Notorious Mrs Ebbsmith*.

The chance to play the Reverend Amos Winterfield had materialised after three years' grind around the provincial circuit. After having put *Bootle's Baby* to bed, Aubrey had toured in a melodrama called *Sin's Angel*, in which he had performed the rôle of what he himself described as a 'questionable hero'. *The Love Chase* followed, and then came the part of Aubrey Tanqueray, resplendent in his Chambers at No. 2X, the Albany, where he surprised his friends when telling them of his plans to marry *The Second Mrs Tanqueray*. At The Theatre, Colchester, where the tour spent a week, Miss Cynthia Brooke, who played the unfortunate Mrs T., was casting quite a spell. 'During the best parts of her acting the audience listened and watched with breathless attention,' trumpeted the local *Gazette*. 'This praise may be nearly fully repeated with regard to Mr Aubrey Smith.'

Well, nearly having given his public respiratory problems whilst playing in the Provinces, Aubrey reckoned that he had served and not been found wanting in a valuable apprenticeship. The reward had arrived. He had been admitted to the West End.

The Notorious Mrs Ebbsmith, quickly lampooned as *The Unsavoury Mrs Dragglejones*, was, in the language of the day, 'the daughter of a sincere demagogue and a pious termagant, who had grown up without having known the joys or caresses of childhood.' Absolutely fatal!

It would be too simplistic to say that the roots of Arthur Wing Pinero's play lay in Mary Wollstonecraft's writings of a century before, and that it was ahead of its time as a sperm for the suffragettes and eventually women's liberation. No such direct connection can be attributed, and yet for the theatre, and as a successor to *The Second Mrs Tanqueray*, it was revolutionary. Here at last, after years of farce and burlesque, was intellectual meat.

The play caused a sensation, and was a vehicle for the towering talents of Mrs Patrick Campbell. 'She spoke and looked like one inspired, and held the house in suspensive awe until one could hear the beating of one's own heart. Heads were stretched forward to catch each word, and "the gods" themselves were hushed.' All the other characters were merely foils for Mrs Ebbsmith and Aubrey was lucky to capture a line in *Theatricals and the River* which noted that he was 'a model specimen of a frank, good-natured, muscular clergyman'. Aubrey admitted that although the part was small he had found it difficult, 'but Pinero has been very kind, and has taken a lot of trouble over me,' and to be on stage in such a company 'even though one may only have to speak a few words, is nothing short of a revelation to anyone who is anxious to improve.'

He was fortunate also in that both Pinero and Hare were avid cricketophiles and, would therefore already have been aware of and interested in his accomplishments. Aubrey was to discover that whenever the hypochondriacal Hare watched a match at Lord's he complained of a draught wherever he sat, even on the hottest of days. Mrs Pat, however, was far from being enamoured of the game, or of Aubrey. 'My God, Joey,' she ranted at George Bernard Shaw, who suggested him for the part of Higgins in *Pygmalion* years later in 1914, 'I can't possibly act with a cricket bat!'

By now Aubrey was used to being 'terribly chaffed', as he put it, by his fellow-actors about his activities as a cricketer, especially when the notices concentrated on that to the exclusion of his acting. He did not let it worry him unduly. *Mrs Ebbsmith* lasted for three months, and Mrs Patrick Campbell for only two before leaving the cast, thereby effectively ensuring that without the production's 'shining light' the remaining run would be short.

Aubrey's next venture was to tour in the title rôle in *The Home Secretary* with Fred Terry, one of the famous theatrical family. Then with Terry, Julia Neilson (Mrs Fred Terry), John Hare, and the Garrick Theatre Company, Aubrey embarked on the first of his many visits to the United States of America.

Hare and Pinero were furious that Beerbohm Tree had enticed Mrs Pat away so soon from *Mrs Ebbsmith* for a production of his own, and ever since the early closure had been negotiating for an American tour which they felt would bring the financial rewards the play deserved. Julia Neilson was to take the rôle of 'Mad Agnes', the Ibsenish woman of independence – 'I've anathematised my womanhood often enough' – and the production was under the direction of Clarence Fleming.

For Aubrey it provided the proverbial 'chance of a lifetime' as they opened on Broadway at Abbey's Theatre on the Monday after Christmas, having spent the holiday on the boat enjoying riotous festivities. He had made a gesture to the 'open-air life' by taking along an enormous bag of golf clubs in lieu of a cricket bag, and in no time he was enjoying the adulation that went with being a member of an English company. The exciting sights, sounds and experiences of New York made even the tat and grime backstage seem full of lustre. The tour, which lasted several months, seemed all too short and soon he was packing happy memories of the visit, together with his golf clubs.

On his return any feelings of anti-climax were quickly dispelled with the preparations for his forthcoming marriage.

Aubrey had known of his wife-to-be, Isobel Mary Scott Wood, through her father, who was a patient of his own father; he had then been introduced formally by a friend, Reggie Baiss, who at the time was her fiancé. Isobel's father, Major Alexander Wood, was one time A.D.C. to General Gordon of Khartoum, and when she married Aubrey, Isobel was in her twenty-third year. She was an attractive girl, with a trim figure, pale complexion, and dancing grey eyes that were framed by curly, red hair. The marriage took place on August 15th, 1896, at All Saints' Church, Belvedere in Kent, not far from her family home at Abbey Wood, and though there was some feeling among her relatives that she was marrying 'down', her immediate family softened the blow by saying that 'dear Aubrey is such a nice man, and has been up at the University, even though he is an actor.'

It would appear that though 'merely a player', in some quarters Aubrey was still considered quite a catch. In her autobiography Dame Irene Vanbrugh recalled that around this time Aubrey was her host on an Eton v Harrow match day at Lord's, and that she 'felt the halo of his great achievements ... he was a very good-looking, charming man, I imagine in the early thirties, and as he handed me a cup of tea I was conscious of the envious glances being levelled at me ...'

Aubrey and Isobel's first home was a basement flat in Trebovir Road, Earls Court, and in relatively cramped surroundings the initial problem was to find room for a grand piano and a St Bernard dog. 'One has got to go,' warned his young wife ominously.

Meanwhile Aubrey had been spending much of his time in rather gruesome theatrical 'digs' around the country, while touring as Black Michael in Edward Rose's adaptation of *The Prisoner of Zenda*. George Alexander had produced the play, and it had also been performed on the recent trip to the States. Aubrey was now becoming acquainted more fully with Alexander, the canny Scot, who, since being in charge of the St James's Theatre, had adopted a successful policy of encouraging British playwrights by providing an outlet for their work. Alexander, who had made the St James's into a smart society theatre, had not suffered from the publicity of a year or so earlier, surrounding his tangle with the police over an alleged sexual misdemeanour with a lady in the street. In fact, business had never been better.

In December 1896, Alexander mounted a three-month run of *As You Like It*. He himself played Orlando, Julia Neilson of the brooding brown eyes and pleasant pout was Rosalind, H. B. Irving played Oliver, H. V. Esmond Touchstone, and Aubrey took the part of Frederick, usurper of the dominions of his brother, the Duke. Incidental music had been specially composed by Edward German, and in 114 performances Shakespeare's pastoral comedy netted £200 a night, a handsome profit. In his review George Bernard Shaw wrote that 'Mr C. Aubrey Smith's appearance is so magnificent that it taxed all his powers to live up to his own aspect.'

Nine days later Pinero's *The Princess and the Butterfly* opened with many of the same players in the cast. In the author's words, it was a play that dealt 'with the struggle of middle age with love', and it is a fair assumption that after a hundred performances of five acts, elaborate scenery and costume changes, differences of opinion between Pinero and Alexander, and a deficit of almost £2,000, that same cast felt that the theme of the play had become autobiographical. Aubrey, in star-strewn company, played Lieutenant-Colonel Arthur Eave.

Aubrey was now afflicted with the 'disease' of every actor, when the pangs of not being able to trouble the Exchequer with employment lasted for five months. Ironically *The Happy Life* signalled his return to remuneration, as the 'legal eagle' Cyril Charteris with chambers at Fig-Tree Court in the Temple. The comedy played at the Duke of York's Theatre which was being leased by the American theatrical manager and producer Charles Frohman, who was to have such an influence on Aubrey's subsequent career. In a few years' time, Frohman, with his brother Daniel, Mark Klaw, Abe Erlanger, Al Hayman, Sam Nixon and J. F. Zimmerman, was to form the monopolistic 'Syndicate' which sought to control theatrical enterprise and distribution throughout America. Nevertheless, the 'Buddha-like' Frohman was always extremely courteous in his dealings, and was generally held in affectionate regard by all with whom he had contact. At one period he controlled five theatres in London's West End.

Unfortunately for Aubrey *The Happy Life* did not last long, and he found that his small savings were being rapidly depleted. With the responsibilities of marriage, he looked for greater security.

He found it as business manager for George Alexander at the St James's. Alexander had committed himself to a heavy touring schedule, and felt that he needed someone he could trust to keep his house in order. Who better than Aubrey with whom he had established a rapport.

While he was running 'the shop' Aubrey inevitably learned a good deal about the traumatic preparation and complicated 'wheeling and dealing' that seems inherent to every major theatrical undertaking. It was an aspect of theatrical endeavour that he did not enjoy, and he was basically far too straight-forward, trusting and lacking in duplicity to have made a success in that side of the business in the long term.

Alexander, however, placed great reliance on his manager. There was one occasion during Aubrey's two years in office when a fire had started in the theatre, and Alexander asked him to go out front, pacify the packed house and quell any signs of panic. A mission accomplished satisfactorily. Towards the end of Aubrey's stint, the theatre was dark for six months to allow for structural alterations and increasing the seating capacity. It was a time when Aubrey felt divorced from the stimulus of the stage.

Around this period, at the turn of the century, the walks on stage that Aubrey had made 'in character' were in *The Ambassador* where, in the light of later rôles, it is surprising that he did not play the lead; Alexander reserved that honour for himself, and Aubrey was happy enough to be Major Hugo Lascelles, and who would not be happy with a residence in the Champs Elysées; *The Man of Forty*, a modern play by Walter Frith in which Aubrey took the part of Algie Portman, a golf maniac who looked decidedly Gallic in appearance, thinning on top, with a droopy moustache, and an acerbic turn of phrase – 'What price my lost ideals ...'; and Hugh Graeme in *The Wilderness*, a comedy by H. V. Esmond which, judging by the nature of the author's introduction, was a gunning platform aimed at his audience. 'I use the name to indicate the general blasé or rather aimless section of so-called High Society; those people who are "wandering" as it were through life. I attempt to show a group of men and women – not vicious or sensual, but who for a time blunder along, so to speak, not bothering about anything worth bothering about, until – until they are made to bother.'

A glance further down the programme revealed real bathos. 'Mr George Alexander earnestly begs his Lady Patrons to remove their hats for the benefit of those seated behind them.'

Nothing is more irksome than the necessity for making a living if it interferes with leisure activities. Aubrey was determined that for him this should not happen. The lure of cut grass and pitched stumps remained strong, and the Actors' Benevolent Fund needed money. What greater justification was needed?

The match at the Oval between London and Provincial Actors was in effect the birth of the Thespids Cricket Club. Frank Benson and Oscar Asche were on one side, and H. B. Warner, Rutland Barrington and Aubrey on the other. An exciting finish was exactly the spur that was needed to set things in motion, and having chosen suitable colours – green and white with purple strip (the suffragettes found them fetching, too!) – found a ground on which to play, the Grange at Acton, and made up a fixture list, Streatham, Surbiton, Virginia Water, Guy's Hospital, Musicians, Playgoers, etc., etc., the only thing left to do was find a side. And often that was more difficult than it seemed. Extra rehearsals, matinées, prior commitments, all messed up the tidiest of plans, and many a 'civvy' or non-acting fill-in was called on at the last moment to make up the numbers.

The Grange was put out to grass after the proprietor's horses took up squatters' rights, and the Thespids moved to St Quintin's Park. Not all the matches were played at home. There was a game against London County at Crystal Palace who had W. G. and Billy Murdoch in their side, and Gilbert Hare and H. B. Warner surprised even themselves by putting on a hundred for the first wicket. Many of their opponents included famous cricketers, some pre or post their peak: Johnny Douglas and Patsy Hendren were two, and even the Thespids lay-members were not short of a distinguished name – W. S. Churchill!

Eventually St Quintin's Park went the way of the Grange and there was a migration to Malden, though the reason for the move this time was that Aubrey had found bits of firewood, corks, pebbles and glass rolled into the pitch. As he wrote in his article for the *Cricketer Winter Annual* in 1921, 'One gets used to pebbles and so on, but corks!'

On occasions, the Thespids called their side the Actors, for instance for the fixture at Lord's versus the Authors, when the literary men were captained by Arthur Conan Doyle and had Philip Trevor, J. C. Snaith and Hesketh Pritchard in the side. The Actors were equally accomplished – Basil Foster, Brian Egerton, Gerald du Maurier, H. H. Ainley and Oscar Asche, who had in his time played Minor County cricket. The bulky Asche, who on the night of one Eton and Harrow match wanted all the robbers in his *Chu Chin Chow* to carry miniature cricket bats on to the stage, was liable to become irascible if an innings was slow. His invective was once turned against J. W. Hearne, who had been labouring somewhat: 'How I would like that fellow to play Desdemona to my Othello, because I should enjoy strangling the life out of his carcass.' One other never-to-be-forgotten Thespidian story concerned Frank Benson, who was heading a stock company in 'the sticks', presenting Shakespeare. He sent a cable to London requesting a cast replacement: 'Send me a slow bowler to play Cassius.'

Aubrey turned in some notable performances for the Thespids. In 1905, in the days when the side carrying their cricket bags hurried past churchgoers rather furtively, he took 10 for 27 against twelve Playgoers, and generations later, when he was nearly eighty, Garry Marsh, who captained the Stage XI for years, remembers him taking a brilliant catch at second slip in a game against Brondesbury. 'The ball was going like a bullet, and his hand just eased out and swallowed it.'

Many of those theatrical outings were for charity, and for a long time Aubrey was honorary treasurer of the Actors' Orphanage. His 'man' Jack Beckett, who helped as stage dresser and general factotum, was nearly always umpire for the Thespids, and he acted in the same capacity for Incogniti as well. Beckett, who was a stocky, warm-hearted Cockney and a cousin of Joe Beckett, one-time British Heavyweight

Champion, was devoted to 'the Guv' and was with Aubrey for nearly thirty years.

Aubrey also played cricket for the West Drayton Club in Middlesex up until the First World War, and in that season when hostilities began and he was in his fifty-first year, he had topped the batting averages. He and his wife had moved home to the village, as it was then, in 1902. At first they had rented Avenue House from the Pankhurst family, which was a lovely old Georgian dwelling just off the Green, and then later they bought five acres of land near the River Colne in Mill Road and built 'Old Orchard'. There were two cottages already in the grounds and eventually, after his mother had died in 1916, Aubrey's father moved into one of them. Before this Aubrey's parents had lived next door in a house that had been bought by their son, who also became responsible for the running costs. These were not inconsiderable, as the staff consisted of a maid, a cleaning woman and a gardener, and there was practically no income from the hands of the doctor, who had now retired and was concentrating on breeding terriers for competitions at Cruft's. By now, Aubrey and his wife had a daughter, who had been christened Honor in the local St Martin's church. Aubrey's sister Beryl had married the novelist Cosmo Hamilton, and they lived just round the corner, so in the space of a few years West Drayton had undergone an invasion of Smiths.

Ever since the move to the meadows of Middlesex, Aubrey's theatrical career had prospered. An engagement with Lillee Langtry (the correct spelling) at the playhouse that was a white elephant, the Imperial (a mixing of species really, as the theatre was an adjunct of the Westminster Aquarium) in *The Degenerates* had started the dice rolling. The Jersey Lily was the sole lessee and manager of the Imperial Theatre, much to her cost, before eventually she and the Wesleyans succeeded in having it pulled down and rebuilt in the East End, where it became a cinema. In *The Degenerates* Lillee, who was then nearly fifty, took the part of Mrs Trevelyan, and Aubrey that of the Duke of Orme. The incidental music included two songs composed by Miss Jeanne Langtry. It is not known whether Aubrey had any ice poured down his neck, though in the programme for the play Mrs Langtry was exercising her penchant for publicity by advertising hair restorer.

Previous to using 'Harlene' my hair had become brittle and was falling off. (Did the Prince of Wales notice, I wonder?) I have used your preparation for 18 months, and my hair is quite restored. I cannot recommend 'Harlene' too highly.

Then in the September of 1902 Aubrey joined Gertrude Kingston at the Comedy Theatre in *Secret and Confidential*, a 'drawing-room melodrama', in which he played the Hon. Henry Challace, described as 'a worthless father with a high collar and waxed moustache, who has sold a State document'. The action of the drama was set in Aubrey's old stamping ground, St James's, and, of course, it is from there that all stenographed secrets fly the nest. Kate Terry Gielgud wrote in a letter that 'only the well conceived and excellently presented picture of the unscrupulous broken-down old gentleman as played by C. Aubrey Smith will live in one's recollection.'

From Whitehall to the Sudan is but a short step in the land of theatrical make-believe. Aubrey had been invited to the War Correspondent's Tent in the North African desert by courtesy of Johnston Forbes Robertson, another old Carthusian in the thespian trade. *The Light that Failed* is about a painter who suffered periodic bouts of blindness after having been shot at in the afore-mentioned Sudan. Actor/manager Forbes Robertson used the first rôle in his duality to create a staggering impression of the artist Dick Heldar, and the 'truest, simplest, and sincerest of friends', Gilbert Pelling Torpenshaw, was admirably played by Aubrey. In the drama there is humour both intentional and unintentional, especially if taken in isolation:

Dick's amour, Maisie (Gertrude Elliot): You're very inconsiderate to keep on at me – you know I can't behave differently till the last scene ...

Bessie Broke (Nina Boucicault), *who is a poor, ill-conditioned little drab but useful as a model, kneels at Torpenshaw's feet:* Couldn't you take and do with me until Miss Right comes along? I'm only Miss Wrong I know, but I'd work my hands to the bare bone for you.

Torpenshaw (Aubrey): It's a biggish world – but it's just full of women.

The play was an adaptation of Rudyard Kipling's novel, and the critics were unhappy about what they considered to be a phoney happy ending, which apparently had been inserted originally for the benefit of the American public. Aubrey had a liking for Kipling, in fact he was enamoured enough to set the *Barrack Room Ballads* to music, which involved no more than a simple interspersion of trumpet calls at significant moments. His musical attributes were never extensive: they comprised a forthright if basic striding of the piano in the best traditions of the Victorian smoking room, a purposeful bass-baritone with the ability to extract the utmost from any comic nuances in the song, a love of Puccini, and an ability to start the pianola.

After a two-month run *The Light that Failed* went out at the Lyric and came on again at the New, and subsequently Aubrey toured with it in Forbes Robertson's company in the United States. Before that, though, he had brought the house down ahead of time at the Imperial Theatre at the expense of George Bernard Shaw. Shaw had mounted a single performance of *The Admirable Bashville* for the sole purpose of establishing copyright. Aubrey, who was playing a policeman, asked the great playwright if he might portray the rôle as an Irishman. Shaw concurred readily enough, and so Aubrey scurried off to Clarkson's, the wig-makers, and transformed himself into an incredibly close resemblance to the dramatist. His appearance on stage produced a standing ovation, or rather everybody either was standing or laughing, with the exception of Shaw's mother who failed to see the joke.

Having successfully spoofed Shaw, Aubrey obviously felt confident enough to face a further foray with Mrs Patrick Campbell, this time at the New. The entire production of the revival of *The Second Mrs Tanqueray*, we are told, was under the management and direction of Mrs Pat. Charles Frohman also received a credit for direction, which for him seems like relegation, and whether he managed to contribute anything is doubtful. Aubrey took his old rôle of Mr T. and nearly forty years later remembered the production vividly. 'What a perfect performance Mrs Pat gave as Paula Tanqueray. Rather! ... Pinero was a great craftsman, wasn't he?'

Aubrey did sufficiently well to be invited back to *Warp and Woof* at the Vaudeville for the next season in 1904, and seeing that there were sixteen other women in the cast, discounting Mrs Pat, and only four other men, he had every opportunity.

The previous September he had taken to the high seas again on board S.S. *Philadelphia* with Forbes Robertson's Company for a tour of the U.S.A. and Canada. The trip was extensive, lasting for almost eight months in cities such as Boston, Cincinnati, Cleveland, Montreal and New York, and the plays presented were *The Light that Failed* and *Hamlet*. A few weeks before the boat sailed Aubrey had been approached by Herbert Beerbohm Tree, who wanted him for one of his forthcoming ventures. He explained that he had accepted an invitation to join the Forbes Robertson tour, and would therefore be abroad at the time, whereupon Tree upped the ante. 'Have you actually signed a contract?' enquired the eminent actor/manager. 'No,' replied Aubrey, 'but I've given my word.'

At the Knickerbocker Theatre in New York Aubrey played the Ghost of Hamlet's father, and anyone less insubstantial or ethereal would be difficult to imagine. One of the players in the company was J. H. Beaumont, who kept everyone amused by drawing humorous sketches caricaturing happenings throughout the tour. Aubrey figured largely in these 'American Sketches More or Less from Life'.

On familiar territory once more at the St James's Theatre near the end of 1905, Aubrey joined Lilian Braithwaite, one of his favourite actresses, in Wilde's *Lady Windermere's Fan*, and as Lord Darlington endeavoured to persuade the Lady Windermere to avenge herself because her errant husband's attentions were elsewhere. The run was twelve weeks, and the box office buoyant.

While still playing Lord Darlington, Aubrey had started the confusing process of learning another rôle, that of Colonel Grey in J. M. Barrie's play *Alice Sit-By-The-Fire*. The production was for Charles Frohman at the Duke of York's Theatre, and Dion Boucicault was directing a cast that included A. E. Matthews, Irene Vanbrugh and Ellen Terry:—

One of the greatest joys of my life was playing with Ellen Terry. When we came to do *Alice Sit-By-The-Fire* she got the script at Christmas, we started rehearsals in February and we rehearsed for six weeks, and at the end of six weeks she knew no more of her part than she did on the day we started ... Ellen was delightful, a darling, but she was a frightfully slow study. That was a family trait.

At one halting moment in the preparation Barrie had given vent to his annoyance. 'It doesn't matter what you say, dear lady,' he expostulated, 'but for God's sake, say something.'

The great actress was not sure of her lines even after the performances had begun. One night in a particularly moving scene Aubrey looked round and found Ellen at the other side of the stage, searching surreptitiously for her cue under her handkerchief. 'If the audience noticed anything, I am sure they thought it was I who was wrong,' said Aubrey.

The following year he was one of three hundred who appeared at Drury Lane in honour of the Ellen Terry Jubilee. The tribute involved play excerpts, recitations, monologues, dances, songs, minstrel groups; a scene from *Trial by Jury*, in which Gilbert himself appeared and Aubrey was one of the crowd; another scene from *The School for Scandal* with George Alexander and Sir Charles Wyndham, and so it went on and on. The colossal cast for this entertainment extravaganza, or mammoth marathon as somebody called it, was a *Who's Who* of stage and variety. Seymour Hicks, Ellaline Terriss, Caruso, Mrs Patrick Campbell, Gertie Millar, George Grossmith, Herbert Beerbohm Tree, Gerald du Maurier, Henry Ainley, Conan Doyle, Zena Dare and A. E. Matthews, who was then a mere stripling. The great tragedienne Eleonora Duse watched from a box, and Ellen Terry herself, who had first appeared on stage at the age of nine, set the seal on the evening by acting in an excerpt from *Much Ado About Nothing*. Presumably her choice was not meant to be a comment on the proceedings.

The fact that Aubrey had been invited to be part of such exalted company showed that by now he had received the hallmark of an established West End name. In the space of fourteen years he had become recognised as an actor of quality, close to the top of his profession. Summaries of his work appeared at various times:

A strong, yet sympathetic and flexible voice, he would dominate almost every scene in which he appeared. It was his good fortune to be cast in sympathetic roles, and it was the good fortune of the audience that his characterisations were given with consummate ease and grace.

Another reads:

There were better actors, but in his own sphere he had no equal. He acted in earnest the sort of part that many other actors play as a joke – the stern, tweedy, pipe-smoking squire type, solid and dependable as a rock.

It is true to say that the theatre of the early nineteen hundreds in the main revolved around drawing-room comedy with its languid world of dukes, dowagers and diplomats reclining in the cushioned comfort of Mayfair mansions, with another seat in the country, and the odd allowable gesture towards a *palazzo* in Venice, especially if it was holiday time. The Army, the Law and the Church were acceptable institutions for gentle guying, and as the characters within their walls helped form the foundations of the Empire, all was understood and forgiven. The theatre was pleasantly patriotic and totally undemanding, and even if there were a few and gradually increasing number of plays with social comment, managers, with an ever-wary eye on their select and by today's standards snobbish audiences, not unnaturally tended to favour the 'safe' commodity. This world of privilege was peopled by certain, easily definable types, who on the whole operated with tailor-made rules and limited compass, and therefore the range of characterisation available to Aubrey was similarly restricted. Apart from that, each actor had and has to contend with the inflexible confines of their personal physique and capacity to 'be' a rôle, and of course that meant for someone of Aubrey's stature there already existed inbuilt boundaries. His authoritative *persona* was realised best on stage in his ability to project himself, and not someone else, and therefore often he was a noble lord and never a humble lackey.

Prior to the Terry celebrations at Drury Lane, Aubrey had attached himself to Arthur Bourchier's Company for a couple of Alfred Sutro plays, *The Walls of Jericho* at the Shaftesbury Theatre, and *The Fascinating Mrs Vanderveldt* at the Garrick. Bourchier, who was generally over-eager and impatient in rehearsals and highly sensitive to any criticism, acted the part of Mr Vanderveldt, and Violet Vanbrugh was the fascination. At least she was for Aubrey, if not for her husband, and although the 'captious critic' of the *Illustrated Sporting and Dramatic News* complained that Mrs Vanderveldt laughed too emphatically and frequently, it was also noted that her old, old friend 'acts with quiet strength and convincing naturalness, the part of the earnest and undemonstrative Colonel Rayner,' and moreover 'cannot be accused of overdoing the smile.'

The Fascinating Mrs Vanderveldt had been co-presented by Bourchier and Charles Frohman, and it was the former who managed Aubrey's next play *The Morals of Marcus*, again at the Garrick, and the latter who eventually invited him to tour with it in the USA.

The play was adapted from his popular novel *The Morals of Marcus Ordeyne* by the author W. J. Locke, and centred on the relationship between Sir Marcus Ordeyne and Carlotta, a waif raised in a Syrian harem. The setting was a cottage in Surbiton. The construction of the piece was berated by the critics, who felt that the minor characters had too little to do with the action, and that the duologue between Sir Marcus (Aubrey) and Carlotta (Alexandra Carlisle) had lost subtlety in the transference to the stage. The principals received mixed notices. Wrote the *Daily Telegraph*:

> Mr C. Aubrey Smith, excellent actor though he be, seems hardly at home in the part of Sir Marcus. Mr Smith is the embodiment of the solid, straightforward English gentleman who lives the open-air life of an all-round sportsman. Sir Marcus he represents as a great, big, kind-hearted school-boy, very shy withall, bewildered and not a little irritated by finding himself unexpectedly confronted by the problem of the eternal feminine. Of the bookworm, of the dreamy philosopher, he offers but the slightest trace: he is a man of action, not of reflection.

The *Graphic* put some of the same things in a different way:

Mr Aubrey Smith has few equals in the delineation of the polished, straightforward, simple-minded English gentleman, and there are no traces of that 'Dingo dog' madness about him of which there should at least be some signs in Sir Marcus Ordeyne. But though it was almost certainly not what the author conceived, there is something striking in the effect produced on the obvious sanity of Mr Aubrey Smith's Sir Marcus by the charm of Carlotta. Had he been more romantic and poetic, his infatuation would have seemed more natural, but at the same time it would have been less of a contrast of character. The subjugation of such a man is perhaps more dramatically effective than if he had been represented as a man more easily swayed by unaccustomed charms.

There was a quibble about pronunciation:

Sir Marcus, being an Englishman, would, of course, pronounce 'harem' to rhyme with 'scare 'em', though Levantines would hardly so do. But these are minor points. The performances of Miss Carlisle and Mr Aubrey Smith are what the public go to see, and they are so out of the common, and so interesting, that they have well deserved success.

And success they had, with the public. They flocked to the performances, and, judging by the applause, seemed very happy with what they had seen.

On the lengthy American tour, which began after an interval of some months, and which covered the Eastern States from Boston to the flooded Mississippi, the part of Carlotta was taken by Marie Doro. Obviously Aubrey approved, as is seen from his interview in 1941 with journalist Ward Morehouse. 'What glorious eyes Marie Doro had – and still has. We saw her recently in Hollywood. She's still exquisite – so tiny and slender. And a fine actress.'

At the time, in October 1907, the author W. J. Locke wrote to Aubrey in New York from his home in Maida Vale. 'I'm glad you like Miss Doro. Her whole heart seems to be in it – but oh! that star system – how rotten it is. And how it must kill the drama ... You know how absolutely identified you are in my mind with Sir Marcus – so wishing you luck in wishing yourself luck.'

The American critics felt that Aubrey carried the whole play, which was thought to be slight. Miss Doro got on their nerves 'by her total lack of repose. If she could only acquire some of the reserve of Mr Smith she would come nearer realising the character of the girl. Innocence is not signified by a body on springs.'

This was Doro's first appearance as a 'star', and according to reports she was 'quite up to the stellular altitude'. W. J. Locke wrote again in the following March: 'Frohman has gone mad over Doro. She's going to play it in Berlin, in Esperanto! Have they suggested you should play Marcus?'

Aubrey's reply is not known. In the interval between the English and American stagings, Aubrey had crammed in three plays. For Frohman, with whom he had an unwritten agreement for first call on his services (around this period if Aubrey worked for other managements it was usually billed as 'by arrangement with Charles Frohman'), he played the Marquis de Tallement who was the *fons et origo* of all the mischief in *The Great Conspiracy* at the Duke of York's. This was a star-studded but unsophisticated Napoleonic epic, and the *Globe* reporter at first hardly recognised Aubrey in his disguise as an old innkeeper, and after 'sympathetic acting of the highest value to the piece', he was quite disappointed to find that he was the villain of the play.

Then Aubrey had crossed swords with the Suffragist Movement in a dramatic tract called *Votes for Women* at the Court Theatre. He played the rôle of a rising politician who had treated a lady abominably, went to say sorry, and found she was 'working for her sex'.

And to complete the hat-trick, and after such a horrid experience at the Court, he had checked in with *My Wife* at the Haymarket, for a romp that began at Mount Street and ended in the Swiss Alps. 'You think you're looking cross, but you're quite mistaken,' trilled Trixie (Marie Lohr) to her husband (Aubrey).

After his return from the arduous trip with Sir Marcus Ordeyne in the States, Aubrey received an invitation to join his old school pal Cyril Maude in a new four-act Naval Comedy that had been written by the team of Drury and Trevor. The energetic Maude, with whom he had played 'tip and run' between classes, had now become one of the great assembly of actor managers, and his theatre, the Playhouse, was preparing to take aboard *The Flag Lieutenant*. The Playhouse, appropriately situated on the Thames Embankment, later led a chequered existence before becoming a B.B.C. Studio, but on the first night in June 1908 it 'struck oil'. The rapt audience heard all about friends saving one another in nasty scrapes, the frightful risks in being surrounded by a horde of Baski-Bazouks, and moral promotion in the eyes of the loved one, having 'done the right thing' after all. Maude himself played the Flag Lieutenant, and Aubrey took the part of William Thesiger, a Major in the Royal Marines who had been passed over in the promotional stakes. After a much acclaimed opening, Aubrey continued to save his 'old chum's honour' three hundred and eighty-one times. As the Flag Lieutenant's wife said to the Major: 'I do love men who do things, who save ships, lead forlorn hopes ...'

Just over a week after the run commenced the audience stood to attention as King Edward VII entered the Royal Box. The play obviously was in the best traditions of the Senior Service, and the King was much impressed for he asked for a Command Performance at Sandringham, and got it in November of the same year. On the night Aubrey nearly knocked over one of the stage guns with his hat, which caused great hilarity amongst the royal audience, but after a dreadful moment of suspense it fell back on to its bearings.

As an actor Aubrey was only too aware of the risks in turning down offers of work, and so a mere three days before the Royal Command he had started playing Adrian White, K.C. in special matinées of *The Builders* at the Criterion Theatre. The next March he adopted the same routine, this time in afternoon theatre at His Majesty's in a play with a title redolent of a Bayswater brothel – *The House of Bondage*. Aubrey was a Harley Street specialist and his sister, Beryl Faber, played the Duchess of Banff; so it could not have been as bawdy as it sounds. Or could it?

Performing in one play in the afternoon and another at night is a schedule too punishing for the majority, yet Aubrey appears to have been unaffected. His next venture, in the June of 1909, was a return to the Playhouse for a bout with *A Merry Devil*, which was a sixteenth-century Florentine farce all about hogs in sacks from which boots protrude. Having buried inanimate bodies that he knew not of, Aubrey betook himself to the continent with which he was becoming increasingly familiar.

A cable had arrived from William Brady, that incredible barnstorming showman, who promoted championship boxing and Shakespearian tragedy virtually simultaneously. Aubrey originally had met Brady, together with his wife Grace George and actor Holbrook Blinn, in London some years before. Now Brady wanted Aubrey to partner his wife (Grace George) in a Stateswide tour of Thompson Buchanan's play *A Woman's Way*. It was to be the longest trek around America that Aubrey had ever undertaken, and the play in tandem with alternative offerings *Diverçons* and *The Best People*, in which Aubrey was suitably aristocratic as Lord Emsworth, gathered enthusiastic houses.

The lure of the States was strong, for back in London Aubrey only lingered for a year before returning to team up in a French comedy with Billie Burke, who was remarkably long-suffering as Florenz Ziegfeld's second wife. Aubrey seemed to be inextricably entwined in a Gallic situation at this time, for two of the three plays in which he had acted during the relatively short spell in London had settings in France. In between a short outing with *Sister Ann* at the Coronet Theatre in Notting Hill Gate, and a jaunt at the Haymarket as Boismartel, President of the Court at Aix in Sardou's *Above Suspicion* (Shaw would have epitomized the well-made play as 'typically Sardoodledom'), Aubrey had resided for a while at the Prince of Wales Theatre in Piccadilly, but really it was all happening at St Lunaire, a fashionable watering-hole in Brittany.

Inconstant George was played by Charles Hawtrey, who also

produced, and Aubrey's lot was that of the philosophical husband, Lucien de Versannes, who said reproachfully to his wife, Micheline, 'Then you're seriously in love? How did it happen?' Micheline replies, 'Like a cab accident!' Lucien was also concerned about George's health: 'I don't want you to catch cold, just because you have been making love to my wife.'

Aubrey's own marriage was a happy one, despite the inevitable 'bumpy rides' of the early days, which made the companionable closeness of their advanced years seem all the more worthwhile. Honor is certain that her father had 'affairs', some of which her mother knew about, and which probably led to one of her migraine attacks. Probably also some of these 'affairs' were fond rather than physical – the limitations of the language of the Anglo-Saxons is never more apparent than when deciding the varying delicate shades of meaning covered by the blanket term 'love' – but overall both Aubrey and his wife had a strong spiritual feeling (in the unreligious sense) for the sanctity of the marriage home.

Now and then Mrs Smith, whom Aubrey called 'Tor' from her political inclinations when young (she retaliated with 'Bootles' and, in later years, 'Boof'), had to repel invaders, 'friends' who seemed to be a little too close for comfort, and Billie Burke was one, though whether the seeds had been sown in *The Runaway*, which played Atlantic City, the Lyceum Theatre on West 45th Street, Manhattan, and elsewhere, is open to speculation. We do know that thirty years later, when Aubrey was asked about this excursion, all he said was: 'Had great fun touring with Billie Burke ... I was particularly impressed with New Orleans. Antoine's is a wonderful place. I must go to that city again.' Which reveals absolutely nothing rather well.

On his return to England, Aubrey found a play by Penrhyn Stanlaws from the French of Henry Kistermaeckers, and in conjunction with his old friend Charles Frohman presented it at the Duke of York's Theatre in the late autumn of 1912. First though the potential pulling power of *Instinct* was examined before the critical eyes of a 'scouse' audience in the Repertory Theatre, Liverpool, where Aubrey was billed as the producer. The action of the play was confined to a period of five hours, and the setting was familiar territory for Aubrey, who also played the lead. In a well-appointed house on Long Island the famous surgeon Bradford Mandover has a clash of 'instincts'. One tells him to throw the dying poet lover of his wife into a ditch, and the other, prompted by years of medical brainwashing, means that he will have to take his coat off and save the man's life. What a dilemma!

Feste in *Theatreland* had some fun with the problem:—

INSTINCT

Bradford Mandover, M.D., F.R.S.,
Was a Surgeon who fully deserved his success,
But domestic romance he was apt for to shirk—
Alas! he neglected his wife for his work.
(And the Deuce is to pay in theatrical life
When your instinct is stronger for wielding the knife
Than for courting your wife.)
So pray what could poor Mrs Mandover do—
Remember that she was theatrical too—
When she met with a Poet both famous and young
With a hobby for Syncope, also a Lung?
(Oh, the Deuce is to pay, he's extremely to pay,
When an instinct for Poets is rather your way
    In an up-to-date play.)
When the Surgeon found out he discreetly lay low—
'To-morrow,' he mentioned, 'to Europe we'll go.'
Though her love for the Poet she wanted to quell,
He must come to her room for a final farewell.
(And the Deuce is to pay when two lovers *pro tem.*
Their instinct for Final Farewells do not stem
    At something p.m.)
When she told her young Poet the meaning of it
He seized the occasion to fall in a fit;
She could hardly ask hubby the patient to see,
So she called in his brother, another M.D.
(And the Deuce is to pay when your brother says:
    'Ow!
I've an instinct that if we don't operate *now*
    He'll have made his last bow!')
This moment the Surgeon selects to walk in,

And here's where the thunder and lightning begin.
'Don't you love me?' 'I fear you!' 'Does *he* love you?' 'Yes!'
'Do *you* love *him*?' '*I* don't know!' 'Woman confess!'
(Oh, the Deuce is to pay when your husband displays
The instinct of Primitive Man in the days
    When brute force was the craze.)
See the problem? Will Primitive Man slash and slay
In the splendid old Antediluvian way,
Or will civilised ethics still govern the heart
That has so strong an instinct for surgical art?
(Well, the Deuce wasn't paid; he was foiled of his plan
When the Surgeon sat down on the Primitive Man
    And prepared to trepan.)
Now, Bradford Mandover, M.D., F.R.S.,
Might have saved himself quite a good deal of distress
If before the stage-curtain rang up on the game
He had purchased a programme and studied the same.
(For when Poets, though talked-of, are not in the cast,
And the scene is a Parlour from First Act to Last,
I've an instinct that most of he danger is past
    And the Deuce is out-classed.)

As *Instinct* ran no more than one hour and twenty minutes
Aubrey quickly realised that for the production in Liverpool a
curtain-raiser was needed, and so, with the help of George
Bernard Shaw, *Press Cuttings* was scissored to size in order to
fit the bill. He was then, however, considerably perturbed
to find *Instinct* was scheduled to run in Liverpool simultaneously with Shaw's *Caesar and Cleopatra*. G.B.S. was
equal to the situation. He wired Frohman in suitably Shavian
fashion. 'God in heaven has given you *Instinct*. Withdraw my
play.'

Aubrey's *Instinct* was well received in Liverpool and after
the run in the West End he toured it with a 'fill-in' called
Margery Marries around the country. In those days to be a
West End actor was to enter a tight circle that was entirely
exclusive to that of the provincial actor. Each *for* his own, *in*
his own backyard. To be a star in London did not mean that
you were known in Manchester, and *vice versa*, and to cross
territories could be disastrous. Many an ego needed massage

after a play acclaimed in the capital sank in depression in Scunthorpe, and many a tale of woe was related with relish by the touring companies who met in the waiting-room at Derby Station on Sunday mornings.

In the midst of these provincial tours Aubrey never missed an opportunity to get on to a cricket field, and as far as he was able he kept in touch with the first class game. In March of the previous year he had advocated fairly radical reforms. The gist of a letter to the magazine *Cricket* was that in order to achieve livelier cricket, first class matches should last two days instead of three, and that to bolster interest in ordinary club games the bat should be narrowed by three-quarters of an inch, with the height of the stumps increased by two inches. 'As an experiment, I would like to see a couple of matches between good elevens played at Lord's in September under these conditions, if M.C.C. can see their way to such an arrangement.'

Aubrey hated slow cricket. 'Why doesn't the damn fellow get on with it! Poking around instead of playing his strokes ...' he would snort in exasperation on a Thespid afternoon, as Syd Dixon plodded away for an hour without making a run. He always was thinking of ways to increase the momentum of the game, particularly if there was an advantage for the bowler. He had originally proposed the idea of taller wickets in a letter to the *Pall Mall Gazette* in 1888, and at one time he was in favour of a fourth stump, which, on reflection, would have led to a lot of early teas.

In March of 1913 Aubrey replayed his role of Torpenshaw in a revival of *The Light that Failed* that marked Forbes Robertson's farewell to the stage. During that final week at Drury Lane, Forbes Robertson was knighted, and there was great emotion in the theatre as he walked down among the audience on the last night. There was another Command Performance, this time in front of King George V.

Aubrey's flirtation with the United States continued. He commuted back and forth every year on luxurious liners, and this period just before and at the beginning of the First World War was one of fairly full employment. In London, at the Globe, he had portrayed Christopher Dallas, a fifty-two year old bachelor (not far from his own age) in *Years of Discretion*, which had settings in New York and Brookline, Massachusetts (just in case he had forgotten what they looked like); he had then gone down the road to the Haymarket in *Driven*, in which he played an M.P. who preferred the House to home, and was kept in the 'dark' side of the eternal triangle by a wife with a limited life span.

On Broadway he had indulged in some 'delightful persiflage' with Maude Adams in an unconvincing play by Barrie that had gone through several titles, and in so doing had been a long time in arriving. *The Legend of Leonora* was the story of a lady on trial for murder, and as Aubrey's next appearance was in *Evidence* for the notorious Shubert brothers, perhaps they had something to do with it. He then, *significantly*, had been in *The Lie* at the Harris Theatre, with a subsequent tour, and finished the sequence with *Our Little Wife*, or *Just for Tonight*, as sometimes it was called.

When war was declared, the Smiths were having a short holiday in Marlow. Aubrey was cycling to the station with Honor when he caught sight of a placard. 'Good God, this is frightful,' he exclaimed, and hurried off to get a newspaper.

Aubrey applied to join the Army, but the authorities were adamant that he was too old to be called-up. At the age of fifty-one, and with hammer toes, the result of tight-fitting shoes that he had outgrown when at Charterhouse, he knew that he had little chance of acceptance, and therefore he was only too pleased when a year or so later the suggestion came for him to join the Artists Rifles Volunteers.

And so it was that after the lights had gone out at the theatre, 2nd Lieutenant Smith donned his uniform and went on the Night Watch at Waterloo and Westminster Bridges. The dark hours seemed interminable, and to keep his mind occupied Aubrey fell back on one of his hobbies. He always had enjoyed painting as an amusing diversion, and so he began to draw a colour sketch of the view from the bridge at Westminster.

Aubrey's time in the Volunteers started in 1916, and lasted for about one and a half years. Just after the beginning of the conflict he had been working in America, and while in Chicago was warned not to play golf on the local links, as in certain areas of the Mid-West there was a solid phalanx of immigrants with a German background. It was in Chicago, too, that he received in the mail the hateful stigma of a white feather, and this upset him dreadfully.

There was another upset of the offing. The *Lusitania* had gone down, and with it the man who had employed Aubrey more than any other, the man with whom he had had the closest of working relationships, and with whom he had formed a friendship that had stood the test of theatrical intrigue and ambition. Charles Frohman was dead.

'I loved C. F. His word was his bond. I did many plays with him, and made many crossings, and I always came without a contract.'

Aubrey had just been persuaded by Frohman to take part in a new enterprise. The Frohman Amusement Corporation now was in the business of making motion pictures – brother Daniel would carry on. For Aubrey, the silent era had begun.

6/ Seen but not Heard

'When I went to work in 1915 for the Frohman Amusement Corporation, under the very excellent direction of George Irving ... our studios consisted of two abandoned churches, one on Tenth Avenue, New York, and the other in Flushing, Long Island. I must say they served the purpose very well. In those days of the movie's infancy, actors were not held in high regard. That we were working in ex-churches somehow boosted our morale.'

Even with the Almighty's approval, conditions were sack-cloth and spartan. There were no luxuries such as stand-ins or doubles, and the hot unfiltered lights made concentration difficult, and exhaustion easy. Edward Thursfield, the *Builder of Bridges*, falls in love with the sister of a youth who steals money to dabble in stocks, and Aubrey, who probably did not wish to be reminded of that sort of thing, played the title rôle with 'telling force and pronounced success'.

Builder of Bridges was the second release for the Corporation, and for Aubrey the first of a series of incursions into this new and exciting medium throughout that steamy, enervating summer; *John Glayde's Honour, Jafferay* (the performance he liked the best), and *The Witching Hour*. Having tasted blood, as it were, with the birth pangs of the industry, Aubrey decided to have a look at what was happening over on the West Coast, and found Theda Bara doing the same thing in a different way as a vampire in *A Fool There Was*.

Hollywood then was a collection of shacks, and virtually consisted of four minuscule stages not much larger than cubicles. In one of these cubicles a death-bed scene was being shot. 'A violinist played melancholy music to make the actress look remote,' recalled Aubrey, 'while great glycerine tears rolled down her cheeks.' This, of course, was the time of Pearl

115

White, who emerged somehow unscathed from *The Perils of Pauline* to continue her adventures in *The Exploits of Elaine*. It also was the time when D. W. Griffiths made *The Birth of a Nation*, when Charlie Chaplin signed a contract with Essanay Pictures for $1,250 a week, and when Aubrey's old flame, Billie Burke, was paid $40,000 for only five weeks' work.

When Aubrey was asked whether he found that stage and screen work clashed, he replied: 'Not in the least, and moreover I consider the screen helps the stage in many ways. Certainly film work is good for an actor's technique – it is distinctly good for one's timing.'

'And the screen method of scene-taking, Mr Smith – do you not find it confusing? So many legitimate actors seem to, after the straightforward system of the stage.'

'It is an incentive to think – to remember details, to avoid foolish little mistakes ... Mind you, the stage takes and always will take precedence. The art of photo-play can never touch the art of the spoken drama.'

Aubrey continued to get offers for film work, but the calls of the theatre were insistent, and it was not until 1918 that he was next in front of a camera, and then it was in England. *Red Pottage* was made by the Ideal Company, and it was among the early tentative steps of the British Film Producing Industry, an industry that was to have many troughs and few peaks. In those days companies came into existence, made a few films, formed new alliances, or sank without trace, all in the space of a few months. Aubrey was to become part of one such speculative venture. In the twenties he, together with Nigel Playfair, Leslie Howard and A. A. Milne, floated the Minerva Film Company, with the idea of making films of Milne's stories with Adrian Brunel directing.

'Oh, it was a failure,' said Aubrey philosophically, 'but although we didn't earn much we learned a lot ...' Much of the filming was done in the garden at 'Old Orchard', Aubrey's home at West Drayton, or in the surrounding districts, and on one occasion a messenger called at the house with a missive for Mr Smith, and failed to recognise Aubrey who was in costume and up a ladder.

Milne, nicknamed the 'Phantom Bowler' due to his practice of hiding behind the umpire while delivering the ball, had written his first film comedy, *The Bump*, in 1920, and in it Aubrey appeared armed to the teeth with rifle and revolver. There were to be several similar 'derring-do' rôles for Aubrey in British films, and one of the few that seems to have survived the erasions of memory and neglect is *The Bohemian Girl*, in which he assumed the *Braggadocio* of a gypsy chieftain. Ellen Terry, Gladys Cooper, Constance Collier and Ivor Novello were in the cast, and the director was Harley Knowles. The companies and the films now are as remote as the medium, those old 'silents' in which Aubrey was seen: *The Face at the Window; Castles in Spain; The Shuttle of Life; Flames of Passion; The Temptations of Carlton Earlye; The Explorer; The Unwanted; The Rejected Woman*; for such groups as Alliance, A.S.T.S., Cutts and Wilcox, and for a few other assemblies where the aspirations were high and the liquidity low, these are but now an archival inheritance.

Meanwhile, for Aubrey, the unreality and artifice of the stage had more shape and substance, even if it had less chance of influencing posterity. After his long stint in America at the beginning of the First World War, he had returned to the Duke of York's Theatre in London at the end of 1916 to take over the rôle of Jervis Pendleton in *Daddy Long-Legs* from Charles Waldron. Henry Miller was presenting the play, and he was filling the vacancy left by the death of Frohman. Pendleton, who is a wealthy patron of a John Grier Orphanage, takes pity on a girl of 'lowly birth', and has her transplanted into a higher social strata. The girl is not allowed to know her benefactor, and having seen only his shadow refers to him as 'Daddy Long-Legs'. Aubrey's physique obviously fitted the part perfectly.

Aubrey was destined not to return to the Duke of York's for another thirteen years when, during the run of a play by Walter Hackett, a great deal of renovation was being carried out in the basement. The floorboards had been pulled up, and Aubrey took great delight in showing visitors the submerged River Cranbourn which ran below, and from which a few flowers were starting to grow.

For the second half of 1917 Aubrey returned once more to his old haunt, the St James's, and renewed his association with Sir George Alexander. He appeared in two comedies, *Sheila* and

The Liars, and a play by Harold Owen called *Loyalty* that was really a pulpit to preach against pacifism. Alexander, dying of diabetes, was in the last year of his reign, and a note in the programme reminded the audience that in some quarters the holds on life were tenuous indeed: 'Hostile Air Raids. The Field Marshal's Order – public will be informed immediately "Take Air Raid Action" has been received.'

A certain new realism in tune with the times found its way on stage as well. *The Knife*, playing rather inappropriately at the Comedy Theatre, was a cheerful entertainment, being a mixture of rape and vivisection. It was a controversial play in which a Dr Robert Manning took not only the law but a knife into his hands 'and rendered impotent two criminals who had outraged his fiancée.' Apparently 'the horrid and harrowing circumstances were rubbed in with a perseverance that endured to the end,' and the theatrical papers found also that 'Mr Aubrey Smith was tremendously in earnest with the distress and the fury of the doctor, and his force carried the play along vigorously.'

Prussia has her Iron Cross – England the Order of the British Empire. Prussia can't help it – England can't help it. It had to be – a bit of ribbon with a vertical or horizontal coloured stripe. Blessed is the giver and the receiver. 'Tis the one touch of nature that makes the whole world kin.

The Title, Arnold Bennett's comedy (showing how some live on less than twenty-four hours a day) was presented by J.E. Vedrenne and Dennis Eadie at the Royalty Theatre. Leslie Howard and Nigel Playfair were in the cast, and so were Eva Moore (Mrs Culver) and Aubrey (Mr Culver).

Mr Culver: Only the simple-minded believe that honours are given to honour.
Mrs Culver: If it's so bad as you make out, Arthur, why do decent people take honours?
Mr Culver: I'll tell you. Decent people have wives, and their wives take them by the nose. That's why decent people take honours.

After trying to refuse *The Title* two hundred and eighty-three times, Aubrey remained at the Royalty for *Caesar's Wife* with one. Sir Arthur Little, K.C.B., G.C.M.G., was British Consular Agent in Cairo at the age of five and forty, and he has just taken unto himself a young Violet, who is all of nineteen summers. Somerset Maugham's convoluted dialogue made the playing anything but simple.

Sir Arthur: I put myself in your hands, Violet . I shall never suspect that you can do anything, not that I shall reproach you for; I will never reproach you – but that you may reproach yourself for.

The young Fay Compton played Violet, and both she and Aubrey continued at Dean Street in Louis Parker's *Summertime*, which was put on in the autumn. The play did not last long, and at last Aubrey would have had a chance to turn the tables on Mrs Patrick Campbell, had he so wished.

As it happened he did not, which was a typically generous gesture remembering that the acidulous Mrs Pat had rejected so vehemently G. B. S's suggestion that he take the rôle of Higgins in *Pygmalion* in 1914. Mind you, Aubrey was in good company, as both H. B. Irving and Matheson Lang had been similarly dismissed within a sniping sentence. Now, however, with a revival scheduled at the Aldwych Theatre, several actors found pressing reasons for being unable to play the Professor opposite an undeniably talented if temperamental actress, who was attempting to take the part of a young Eliza Doolittle, while she herself was at the wrong end of her fifties, and in all too obvious physical decline. Her era had passed, she was on the way out.

In the opening weeks of a chaotic rehearsal period, Mrs Pat still continued to tease Aubrey about his cricketing proclivities, that is, on the few occasions that she condescended to attend. 'Good morning, Aubrey dear,' she would carol, as she flounced into view, 'have you brought your cricket bat with you?' Mrs Pat and Shaw were not on speaking terms, which was par for the course as far as her relationship with directors went, and often she would not arrive until four in the afternoon, when she would thrust her face round the door, thumb her nose at

G. B. S., and disappear. Aubrey, who had been filming in *The Face at the Window* (not Mrs P.'s, to everyone's relief) and had more 'silent' commitments on hand (he was juggling rehearsals, and had arranged to miss some of *Pygmalion's*), found the whole thing tiresome and, most unusually for him, was less than line perfect.

In the end Shaw had had enough. He vanished on an 'Irish walkabout' and was absent for the last week before the opening, which gave an unexpected opportunity for Mrs Pat to re-direct parts of the play to suit herself. Amazingly, *Pygmalion* received reasonably good notices. Aubrey, on the other hand, did not. 'Mr Aubrey Smith takes up the late Sir Herbert Tree's role of Professor Higgins, but fails to evolve any definite character from it beyond that of a rude red-headed fellow,' wrote one critic.

The *Daily Telegraph* was in agreement at great length:

> If we were tempted to find in Sir Herbert's Professor something a little too gentle and delicate, Mr C. Aubrey Smith goes to the other extreme. Henry Higgins, in his hands, becomes a brusque, practical and plain-spoken individual wholly devoid of any sensitiveness regarding other people's feelings. What in his predecessor was the outcome of pure absentmindedness is transformed by him into sheer boorishness. The change is certainly not for the better, and tends to deprive the character of the sympathy which would otherwise be extended to his treatment of the aspiring Eliza.

After the first night on the 10th February, 1920, Shaw wrote to Aubrey:

Dear Aubrey Smith,

You wiped the floor with the end of the fifth act handsomely last night; and if you do it again tonight you will have a triumph. But do not say '*My* Galatea': it spoils the point. I am not sure that it would not be better to say 'Galatea, by George!', for it has only just come into his head that he has done the Pygmalion trick and made a woman. But 'my Galatea' implies that there are half a dozen Galateas and that he is in love with this one, which is just the fatal misunderstanding to be avoided.

I have a few notes of the earlier scenes.

In Act I you said 'What a horrible sound!', whereas what he means is 'what a delightfully interesting sound', as if he had captured a phonetic treasure. Cheltenham, Harrow and India got cut out; but that was not your fault.

In Act II the words 'I cannot charge myself with having ever uttered it' will not come right on a high note. Drop to your basso profundo, and say it with indignant solemnity and intense conviction. The words 'I may do these things in a fit of absence of mind; but surely &c.,' are not quite disconcerted enough: there is a sort of messy helplessness wanted, like a child excusing itself, to give contrast to the outburst about the benzine.

In Act III, the change to 'besides, she's useful' is not quite expressive enough – expressive of untidiness, I mean.

In Act IV shew much more sternness when she throws the slippers, and make the hauling of her up from the floor appear as summary and unsympathetic as you can without hurting that game knee of hers. And rub in 'Thank God it's all over', and the boredom, without stint.

In Act V the business of putting your feet up on the harpsichord looks bad from the front: Mrs Higgins would never have stood it. Could you manage to use the chair instead? And do not turn away from Eliza on the motor bus: she can't get the effect of her reply (though she is fool enough to think she can) if you let her go.

That is all. It amounts practically to nothing in such a long and difficult part.

I can't say how sorry I am that you have been worried as you have been through these rehearsals. With a less magnanimous leading man the production would have been impossible. Next time I shall provide you with a more amiable heroine. We were neither of us born to keep the lid on hell.

Ever,
G. B. S.

From the scorings-out in the letter it was obvious that Shaw had tried several versions of that final sentence before finding something suitably vindictive. After two months the play transferred to the Duke of York's, but Aubrey did not stay long in the cast. He took himself off for a short stay in the Sin Parlour of John's Country Place in *Why Marry*, and then waited at the Comedy for *The Ruined Lady* in which the assistant stage manager was a young Nigel Bruce, who was to become part of his future.

Pygmalion's run was not protracted in a new theatre, and with Frank Celler in place of Aubrey. In a letter to his favourite 'flower-girl' Shaw was to wonder: 'Did Aubrey make all that difference?' In fact, it was rhetorical question, because already he knew the answer. Aubrey had written to him offering the chance to take up some film shares, and an invitation to write a screen scenario. Shaw's reply is revealing:

Dear Aubrey Smith,
    I shall not take shares in the films, because it is frightfully inconvenient to be both a workman and an employer in the same trade; besides, who would lend me the money? But if ever I have time I may try to do an original scenario, and then we can talk the matter over.
    It may interest you professionally to know that the effect of your withdrawal from the cast of *Pygmalion* was to drop the business from eleven hundred a week to five! Your market value is therefore £599-19-11 a week.
    I kept away from the Duke of York's ánd allowed Stella to produce it in her own way; and a very sweet and mildly amusing performance is the result.

Ever,
G. Bernard Shaw
P.S. All sorts of events have prevented me from answering your letter sooner; but you will forgive me.

It was in *The Ruined Lady* at the Comedy that the noted munitions factory worker and writer of autobiographical books, Naomi Jacob, made her début as Julia the cook. She was to recall later how in one of the scenes Aubrey had to throw a lemon for her to catch, and often he would hurl it with a twist, or probably just a touch of off-spin. She invariably caught it, and always he beamed with approbation.

Nineteen twenty-one was the year in which Aubrey made his

last appearance at the St James's Theatre. *Daniel* was French, and an opium smoker who needed a doctor, and Aubrey was the locum who answered his need. Sarah Bernhardt, of the 'golden-bell' voice, made her final appearance in London; she was on her last legs, and unable to move about the stage. *Polly with a Past*, which followed, was an American comedy by George Middleton and Guy Bolton and had a glittering cast including Noel Coward, Donald Calthrop, Edna Best and Edith Evans, with Aubrey condemned once more to reside in a Country House on Long Island as Prentice Van Zyle.

He was not allowed to be sequestered in such comfort for long, as rehearsals had started for a play with a topical slant. The Readean Company (Alec *Rea* and Basil *Dean*) were presenting Clemence Dane's new piece, *A Bill of Divorcement* at the St Martin's Theatre, and Dean, who later did so much for ENSA in the Second World War, was to fill the function of producer as well. The premise of the plot was that the recommendations of the Majority Report of the Royal Commission on Divorce had become law. Briefly, the recommendations revolved around the acceptance of divorce on the grounds of insantiy, and Aubrey was cast as one Gray Meredith, who has plans to marry Margaret Fairfield (Lilian Braithwaite) who has divorced her husband, who is in a mental institution. The husband (Malcolm Keen), however, returns home miraculously cured after fifteen years away, and there lies Margaret's predictable predicament. What does the poor lady do? Fortunately, daughter Sydney comes to the rescue, sacrificing her own love to look after her father, and it all ends if not happily ever after, at least with a number of intriguing question marks for the audience to ponder over as they leave the theatre.

The part of Sydney Fairfield was taken by the immensely gifted Meggie Albanesi, whose tragic early death was a great loss to the theatre, and in fact she was ill with influenza until the two dress rehearsals for this play. Scenes in which she appeared had been run through previously in her bedroom, and with both Lilian Braithwaite and Aubrey having other theatrical engagements, the organisation of rehearsals had been extraordinarily deranged.

At the end of a first night in which each of the players performed to the limit of their capacity and at which there was no hint of their lack of proper rehearsal, the authoress came on stage to a volley of cheers. 'I have to thank,' she said, 'a band of magicians who have converted ink and paper into flesh and blood.'

The critics thought that Aubrey made 'the prospective husband the one really strong character in the play, who at the critical moment is not averse to the adoption of stern, even bullying tactics in order to keep the wife from hysteria.' *The Bill* had 401 hearings, and gained great public approval.

Aubrey now assumed rôles with a great deal of decoration. He had, of course, played many parts of distinction with distinction before, but for his next three impersonations he became in turn a J.P., was an F.R.S. with a D.S.O. to boot, and was dubbed K.C.B. The first took him to a Lodge in Buckinghamshire by courtesy of an A.A. Milne comedy *Mr Pim Passes By* which featured Dion Boucicault; the second was set in a Garrison town in Hajristan with *The Green Cord* and had Felix Aylmer as Sir Mortimer Isleworth while Aubrey was Colonel Sylvester Starling; and the third was a bad play called *Glamour*, which was lucky to have ten performances, and in which Aubrey's understudy as Sir George Knowsley was a youthful Raymond Massey. In his book *A Hundred Different Lives* Massey recalls how on one occasion, when he was playing a mid-week matinée out of town with Aubrey, the audience numbered six to the company's seven. Somebody pointed out that they remembered one night acting in a company that had been outnumbered two to one by the paying public. 'What was the play?' enquired Aubrey. '*Henry IV Part II*,' was the answer. 'Good God, sir, that play has a cast of thirty – two to one means an audience of fifteen. Ours is the victory – by a margin of nine, sir, nine!'

Aubrey also made a habit of practising his golfing shots in the wings while waiting to appear. He would use a stick and a ball of paper, and at one performance he chipped the ball through a window of the set right on to the stage . He was distraught, though Massey whispered that no one would notice. Aubrey's stage-whispered reply nobody could fail to notice: 'I know, but I shanked my shot!'

For *Plus Fours* at the Haymarket, Aubrey was joined on stage in the West End by his daughter Honor, and signed her autograph book 'Our first effort together'. Sir Charles Hawtrey produced – he was to die later in that year of 1923; on stage he had perfected the *dramatis personae* of the 'consummate liar', and off stage he capped every occurrence with a text from the Bible. The play was about misrepresented identity, with Aubrey, as novelist Mark Maturin, having his job done for him by a secretary. It had eighty-six performances.

Seven years had passed since Aubrey had been last in America, and this time he journeyed at the behest of the strong-willed David Belasco. Belasco, one of the outstanding names in American theatrical history, had fought long and hard to break the stranglehold of the Syndicate. He had been a first-rate producer, and was meticulous, dedicated, vain and, according to some, untrustworthy. In the past a few authors had regretted leaving their manuscripts for any length of time. Sixteen years before W. J. Locke had warned Aubrey in a letter to read a play to Belasco and not to leave the script: '... he hesitates at nothing ... careful in dealings with him as he is quite unscrupulous.'

Now, however, with the famous manager presumably more hesitant at the age of seventy, Aubrey was to appear at the Belasco Theatre on West 44th Street, New York, in St John Ervine's comedy *Mary Mary, Quite Contrary*. Minnie Maddern Fiske was the illustrious lady chosen to represent the vagaries and caprices of a middle-aged actress involved in some satirical episodes at a conventional English country house, and the *New York Tribune* felt that she gave a 'bright, staccato and suavely ironic' performance, and 'she stays out all night with old Sir Henry Considine (Aubrey) in a skiff upon the ocean.' What more could the burghers of Broadway want?

The play also stopped off at Baltimore and Pittsburgh, and while there Aubrey became quite ill. He had picked up a leg infection after being bitten by a bug that had nestled in dirty theatre boards; it had affected his lymphatic system and spread to the throat. He requested a week off from the play, but the management were adamant in refusing, their own metabolisms being attuned only to the cash register. Aubrey's wife Tor had initially applied ice pack and hot poultice alternately to reduce the leg wound, but finally in desperation, as Aubrey's throat became worse, she called a doctor, who had no option but to lance his quinsies at the side of the stage.

Aubrey was not allowed to forget the rôle of an invalid, as back in London at the Comedy Theatre he next appeared in a wheelchair as Edwin Latter, the Egyptologist who had been lamed by a knife thrown in a dark temple. The *Theatre World* called *The Creaking Chair* 'the best mystery play of the season' and in the cast were Fabia Drake, Sam Livesey, Nigel Bruce and Tallulah Bankhead.

In just over a year Aubrey had teamed up with two of the most attractive and in-demand ladies of the theatre. Peggy O'Neil had been in *Plus Fours* and she had had a hit song written about her called 'That's Peggy O'Neil'; and now Tallulah, who was literally mobbed at the stage door each night, in a thriller that drew the public to three successive theatres, with the Little and then the Vaudeville completing the run of 235 performances.

Having so recently discovered how heartless managements could be, Aubrey perhaps thought that in future he would be safer rather than sorrier if he became one of their number himself. He had joined J. E. Vedrenne and Martin Sabine in producing *The Creaking Chair*, and therefore halfway through the rehearsals, when he felt the package needed tightening up, he had asked Gerald du Maurier to do the job.

Du Maurier was precise and exacting. Miss Bankhead was not overjoyed with some of his directorial suggestions. The tension was just about ready to be lacerated by the proverbial blade when Aubrey stepped in. 'Thanks Gerry old boy, I think you've done wonders, and I can see exactly what you mean, and I expect you're busy ...' 'Yes, I'm damn busy at the moment,' expostulated du Maurier as he strode out through the door. Aubrey walked on to the stage and handed a glass to the irate lady. 'Smash that, Tallulah, and you'll feel much better, won't you.' 'Oh, Aubrey, aren't you—' Crash! The glass shattered in small pieces, and another kind of peace reigned once more. Inside the self-mocking, grandiloquent, more often sultry or viperish manner, Bankhead had a heart as soft as beeswax. Many a stage-door hand would bear evidence to her generosity and kindness in time of trouble, and it is more than a pity that some of her innate warmth found it so hard to gain an exit.

While *The Creaking Chair* was still at the Comedy, Aubrey had welcomed his old cricketing confrère, Sir Home Gordon, Bart, to his dressing-room. 'No wonder there is creaking at the thought of how many more wickets I ought to have taken,' remarked Aubrey with a twinkle in his eyes, 'as I would, had catches never been missed.'

For a few years after his sixtieth birthday Aubrey had ceased to play cricket. He still immensely enjoyed watching the game, and the Thespids still were in intermittent swing; Owen Nares, Desmond Roberts, and the comic O'Gorman brothers who were keen enough to travel from as far away as Newcastle for a match on Richmond Green. 'Late again,' Aubrey would bellow in high good humour as they dashed on to the field, having successfully overcome the vagaries of the Great Northern Line. But with the cares of management heavy on his shoulders, and a few rheumatic twinges in other parts, Aubrey was to admit later in Hollywood that for a time he felt his age, and put his pads away, and that it was the Californian sun eventually that rejuvenated the juices.

The venture into production with Martin Sabine was to prove not only unrewarding, but nearly calamitous. By arrangement with the Gattis they presented *Possessions* at the Vaudeville. Sam Livesey, Ian Fleming, Fabia Drake, Ernest Mainwaring and Matthew Boulton, who also acted as stage manager for Messrs Smith and Sabine, were in the cast. After that they mounted a farcical comedy called *Mixed Doubles* at the Criterion Theatre. Many of the same faces were involved, though Faith Celli, Yvonne Arnaud and Aubrey's daughter, Honor, were new. The characters were described as neither immoral nor amoral, but rather the cheerily philosophical victims of circumstance, and Aubrey gave 'the perfect picture of a perplexed "pukka Sahib" with shattered scruples concerning marital duty and desire'. The acting of all was praised unanimously, though Mr Sabine's production was 'nit-picked'. 'Flawed in small details,' thought 'Yorick' of *Theatre World*:

Do country parsons wear trouser clips in parishioners' drawing-rooms? Would a young diplomat sit about in dusty and begrimed motoring overalls? (et cetera, et cetera). Really Mr Sabine these little things surely wouldn't be done. And it's no defence to say it's all a farce, for these sartorial anactionisms are sheer tragedies, in an age when the tailor makes the man and Oxford trousers mask the coming wo-man.

The next progression for the partnership of Smith and Sabine, if it could be so described, was to take a piece by Joan Temple, a dramatist new to the West End though not to the States, and put it on at the tiny Ambassadors Theatre. *The Widow's Cruise* was labelled 'an atmospheric problem comedy' and the strong pattern of the plot was to show the influence Italy had on a quintet of Anglos. Laura Cowie, Nicholas Hannen, Joan Maude, May Congdon and Aubrey – all were directed on Capri by Martin Sabine, and the scenic realisation of the island and the villa was the work of designer Reginald Hargreaves. *The Cruise* was not to last many weeks, and it is interesting to note that a few months later *Theatre World* was featuring a profile of Aubrey, in their series of 'Entr'actes' written by that same Reginald Hargreaves. As an *avant-propos*, Hargreaves quoted Michel Eyquem, Sieur de Montaigne: 'I speak truth, not my belly full, but as much as I dare.'

There are moments when I could almost wish to be endowed with the attributes and reactions of the opposite sex, if only so that I could experience that wonderful feeling of relaxation and security obtainable within the encircling shadow of that colossal effigy of correctitude which is Aubrey Smith. How splendid to have an all-enveloping respectability infused into one by simple contact! And think of the relief of being allowed for once to abandon the position of 'on guard'.

For the prime virtue of respectability is its power to project an aura of *safety*, and Aubrey Smith is the father and mother, the grandfather and grandmother of all things correct and respectable. It is through this characteristic that he has become the ideal exponent of the pipe-chewing-Dick-Bill-or-Jim-named 'deceived husband'. He was born to smell of tobacco and Harris tweeds, and to wave portentous eyebrows, and blunderingly misunderstand the stammered confession of some 'dear little woman', who had wilted away from his ruthless conformity for the moment in an uncontrollable longing for the exotic. For this last he could never hope to attain, and I doubt if he knows how to be even momentarily atavistic. Such things simply 'aren't done'. And that which is not done will never be performed by Aubrey Smith. He much prefers to go on forgiving women for being in the wrong, and being pardoned himself for being in the right!

It would seem that life is bound to be a little hard on the wielder of a straight bat, since women demand such protean qualities in their men folk. They must be Palladian, cave-man, archangel, rake and babe – all wrapped up in the same skin. That is why Aubrey Smith will have to go forever playing that which is within the limit of his comprehension – the plain decent *sahib*, whose rectitude puts a premium on deception so that he may thereafter blunder in where angels would fear to tread – until dotage takes the spring from his knees and there is no strength left in him with which to lift the weight even of a single eyebrow. Women will always adore him, because he is the perfect example of the type they can bamboozle and twist round their little fingers to their hearts' content. He stands for all that is most essentially British; that queer admixture of sportsmanship, dunderheadedness and sentiment which has rendered the inhabitants of these isles the most exasperating enigma with which any other nation has ever had to cope. Well, well; it is to be supposed that we all have our particular destinies bound about our foreheads.

As a manager he does not shine conspicuously, since in his choice of plays – in these 'four-cylinder days' – he seems to be actuated by a sense of selection that works on one cylinder only. Undoubtedly an actor to be cast by a detached intelligence.

It is tempting to conjecture a reason for such a subtly scathing appraisal, and perhaps it is to be found in an episode that occurred around that time. One day Aubrey's daughter, Honor, bumped into the dramatist, Joan Temple, in Shaftesbury Avenue. Joan told her that the scenery from her play was no longer in the dock in the theatre, but being used elsewhere out on the 'road'. The implications of this were serious, because it meant that Aubrey was paying out rent for scenery supposedly housed at the theatre, whereas in fact he should have been recouping in fees for its loan on tour. Martin Sabine must have instigated the move and, not having told Aubrey, must be pocketing all the proceeds himself.

Honor hurried along to the theatre and related the news to the ever loyal Jack Beckett, Aubrey's dresser. 'What are we going to do about it, Jack?' asked Honor. 'Let's get that blighter Sabine,' replied the redoubtable Jack. 'I'll stand by here and I won't let him get out of the door, Miss Honor, and you tell your Dad what's happened when he comes in.' Sabine arrived, and so did her father, and both were in Aubrey's dressing-room when Honor popped her head round the door. 'Oh, hello, Mr Sabine – Daddy, I met Joan Temple this morning,' Honor cast a quick glance at Sabine, 'and she tells me the scenery's out – it's out, on the road.' 'Oh yes, Aubrey,' interjected Sabine rapidly, 'I forgot to tell you – isn't it lucky?' 'Yes,' said Honor, 'did you forget for a whole two months, Mr Sabine?' 'Honor, don't be rude!' reprimanded Aubrey sternly.

However, the truth emerged gradually, and Aubrey had to accept the fact that Sabine had been less than honest. He was always extremely reluctant to think ill of others; it was an admirable trait that had got him into trouble in the past, and made him singularly vulnerable in the ruthlessly competitive fiefdoms of theatrical enterprise. He was too trusting, and took people at their word, finding it hard to believe that anyone could be less honourable than he was himself. It must have been an unpalatable fact for Aubrey to realise that whenever he ventured into business arenas he emerged severely burned – the world sometimes is a very unfair place.

Hargreaves had designed the scenery for *The Widow's Cruise*, and he may have heard of its 'travels', possibly not realising that Aubrey was unaware of the situation. Righteous wrath needs an outlet: where better than the printed page?

As a result of his dealings with Sabine, who later found himself on the wrong side of the law, and after an unwise investment in a play that failed, Aubrey arrived in New York, in his own words 'down and out at the age of sixty'. Sixty-three actually, but let us not quibble. He still had his house at West

Drayton, which was shortly to be sold, a life insurance, and very little else. Before leaving England he had lingered for a while with *Caroline* at the Playhouse, in the company of Irene Vanbrugh, Marie Löhr and Edith Evans. The play was a Somerset Maugham three-acter, and Aubrey had been 'everything that he should be in the rôle of the bewildered suitor, who finds to his dismay that he has won his heart's desire.'

In America he stayed with Maugham, or rather with his writings. *The Constant Wife*, with Ethel Barrymore catching stage fright on the first night in Cleveland, came to Aubrey's rescue temporarily. George Cukor, who was new to directing then, hid in the fireplace and prompted Ethel as she struggled through her part of Constance Middleton, and Maugham, suffering agonies in the audience, was not placated afterwards when Miss Barrymore flung her arms round his neck saying: 'Darling, I've ruined your play, but don't worry, it'll run for two years.' It did just that, after moving to the Maxine Elliott Theatre in New York, though Aubrey was to desert *The Constant Wife* for *The Bachelor Father* before the run ended.

Edward Childs Carpenter's comedy was to be Aubrey's passport to his third and most remembered career, in the dream factory that had materialised on America's West Coast, and that now was being given fresh impetus with the advent of 'the talking picture'. *The Bachelor Father* was a touch risqué for the time, and Aubrey, as Sir Basil Winterton, V.C., K.C.B., K.C.M.G., who had three unsanctioned children all by different mothers, stole every newspaper headline and all the kudos. The play was to be part of his life for the next two to three years, from the Belasco Theatre in New York to the Hollis Street Theatre in Boston, a tour around the States, a triumphant return to England at the Globe after a week at Golders Green Hippodrome, and later transfers to the Strand and the Garrick, everywhere they went the trumpets sounded. 'He suggests all that the part demands in the highest degree. He is the old regular war horse to his finger tips, with his gusts of explosive anger due to long sojourning in the East, his lovable *volte-faces*, his innate simplicity almost childlike, and under it all a heart of gold, and an undying love of the spirit of youth,' reported N. H. in *Theatre World*.

Sydney Carroll of the daily press was positively eulogistic:

'All, all are gone, the old familiar faces.' So runs the verse written by that immortal essayist and lover of the theatre, Charles Lamb. But, thank heaven, not all of them have passed. However frequently we may sigh for a return of the good old days of the theatre of twenty years ago, we may receive consolation from the thought that not a few of the old brigade are happily left amongst us still. One of the best liked, the most cheerful and most welcome, Mr Aubrey Smith, has just returned to England after an all too prolonged absence in the United States.

Surely never was there on the English stage a more finely polished, a more manly figure, or a greater master of the higher comic spirit. Mr Aubrey Smith has a richly avuncular if not paternal personality. Watching this consummate comedian at the Globe the other night in this crudely funny American play, I could not but be reminded of Charles Wyndham in his prime. No one could have given a richer, more persuasive, or more genial performance. He has to represent an innately objectionable blackguard, but all the coarseness of the character was effectually concealed by the actor's art.

THE TRUE SPORTSMAN

Mr Smith brings to his task all the virtues and idiosyncrasies of the real Englishman. He is tall, broad-shouldered, spare, wiry, big, and pleasant-featured, leonine of head. He has a superlative confidence in himself, an easy, complete mastery of his job. Without an atom of side or conceit he steps on to his stage and joins the scene with all the plasticity of a professional cricketer on a good pitch. Watch his survey of the other characters, that air of overpowering good humour, that look of supreme benignity – of superior wisdom. He suggests the lover of a good cigar, a glass of old port, and a ride to hounds – every form of open-air sport. One longs to see this long-shanked cavalier flashing a foil or sabre.

Aubrey Smith is an actor of the personality school. To my

mind he has never really been valued by the critics at his full worth. Nor has the public put him in the high position to which he is by nature, by training, by experience, and by his natural talents clearly and completely entitled. Unfortunately in the past he has achieved a reputation for being that unluckiest of beings, a 'Sound and reliable actor'. His infallible good breeding, his clean, stalwart, fresh, and vigorous bearing have qualified him to succeed in so many supplementary and secondary parts in which passion has been out of place and in which emotion and all those more thrilling notes that make for success on the stage are banished or belittled.

DANGER OF TYPE CASTING

It is practically impossible for an artist of such definite strongly fixed personality to achieve anything considered by critics or public as abnormally excellent. He is condemned always to be more or less himself. But stop and consider what a wonderful and gracious self that is! How kindly, how friendly, how noble, and how thoroughly sporting a person! Reflecting as I must do on the obstacles in his career, I am driven to moralise on the danger of this modern casting for type – danger not only to the player but his profession.

Here we have a superb performer who, for the greater part of his life, has been relegated by type-casters to second-rate parts and second-class positions, when he should have been recognised continuously by all as a star of the first magnitude. Mr Smith in his time has played many star parts, and played them magnificently, it is true. He has every right to consider himself a leading actor, but do the public as a whole recognise this? Personally, I regard his work as so finished in quality, so full of charm, so distinguished, so authoritative, that I must always put it on a very little lower plane than that of Charles Wyndham's, and upon a considerably higher plane than that of George Alexander's.

America, with her keen, lively and intelligent appreciation of good character acting, has taken him to her heart for far too long a time to please us. It was small wonder that she loved him overmuch, for he is something that she cannot possibly produce for herself – an *English gentleman*.

In the December of 1929 Aubrey was an English gentleman at night and an Irish General in the afternoon, as the Garrick was housing matinées of *Paddy, the Next Best Thing*. Apparently he was wise enough to abandon early the attempt at 'Hibernian enunciation', and considering he was playing opposite the Americanised Irish of Miss Peggy O'Neil, who could blame him? A further lesson at the Duke of York's, and later the Whitehall on *The Way to treat a Woman* brought his English theatrical career to an end. Across the water, however, the spotlights were flickering on, and the sound stages were being tuned in.

'Quiet everyone! – Action!' Aubrey was ready to go.

7/ The Grand Old Man of Hollywood

Aubrey could see the Central Casting Office across the sidewalk from his hotel window. Already he felt at home. The St Francis was comfortable, the weather was warm, and so was the welcome.

It was all happening. George Cukor had made *Grumpy*, Charles Ruggles was *Charley's Aunt*, Ronald Colman *Raffles*, and Eddie Cantor continued to make *Whoopee*. Edward G. Robinson had heralded the start of the Warner gangster era with the line, 'Mother of God, is this the end of Rico?', and even if John Gilbert was forced eventually to remain 'silent' the billboards proclaimed that Garbo had spoken; 'Gimme a whisky with a ginger ale on the side. And don't be stingy, baby.'

Hollywood did not yet look like up-market Ilford; the streets, if not tinged with gold, at least bore a faint resemblance to the best brass, and a fortune there was in the making if the seeker were young, well-built, good-looking, possessed of charm, a distinctive voice, the indefinable 'star' individuality; if he were lucky, and, above all, prepared to make obeisance at the high altar of Moguldom. The East European immigration 'sans rabbis and Talmud' demanded sacrificial offerings, as grist to the megalomaniac mill purveying pulchritude to the multitude. 'Get in there fast sweetheart, there's a crash on the way!' Wall Street was yet to fall on Hollywood, though the shadows were starting to form. At the end of 1930, there still was a year or so's grace.

Aubrey was in the fortunate position of being asked to attend. Hollywood wanted him, and not the other way round. *The Bachelor Father* had created enormous interest and now M.G.M. requested 'C. Aubrey' to recreate his rôle on film.

It was the beginning of an extraordinarily fruitful period of

135

his life, which, harnessed with what had gone before, was to place him on a unique pedestal. Aubrey had reacquainted himself with filming techniques in those last few months in England with *Such is the Law, Contraband Love* and *Birds of Prey,* which R.K.O. were to distribute later as *The Perfect Alibi,* and now here he was in California in the M.G.M. lot with Ray Milland, Marion Davies, the mistress of the newspaper magnate William Randolph Hearst, and Robert Z. Leonard, the director who has been described as 'capable of bringing a fond light to high-class cheesecake'.

'Acting never changes very much, my boy,' said Aubrey to *Picturegoer*'s special correspondent, while refilling his pipe. 'Even the introduction of sound has not radically affected a player's work. A good stage actor made a good silent picture actor, and a good silent picture actor made a good talking picture actor, except in some cases where a defect in the voice made a difference.'

The cameras rolled, and did not stop for Aubrey who, with a contract signed by Louis B. Meyer, just went from one lot to another in the next few years, and literally never ceased to be in work. From the day that Aubrey saw off Alfred Aloysius to the African jungle in *Trader Horn* to the time he caught sight of stenographer Claudette Colbert on a park bench in *The Gilded Lily* was just over four years, and in that span Aubrey had taken a part in nearly fifty films: films such as *The Man in Possession* with Robert Montgomery as the romantic lead, *Daybreak* with Ramon Novarro and Jean Hersholt, *Polly of the Circus* with Clark Gable, *Love Me Tonight,* one of the deftest cinematic comedy musicals ever made, directed by Armenian emigré Rouben Mamoulian and with Maurice Chevalier, Jeanette Macdonald and Myrna Loy finding their voices enhanced by the music of Rodgers and Hart; and then *Trouble in Paradise,* which connoisseurs described as 'one of the gossamer creations of Lubitsch's narrative art', and which had Cary Grant as one of the contract players available for uncast parts. In most of the films during those years, Aubrey was chief supporting player, a character rôle in line with the image he presented to the world, aristocratic, lordly, avuncular, authoritative and the like, though there were exceptions as we will see later.

For *Daybreak* (revealing improved photography with super-sensitive Eastman film), which was an elegant romantic fable about an Austrian guardsman falling in love above his station, it was necessary for the five leading men to display a sound knowledge of Austrian army drill. Jacques Feyder, the director, had hired a Captain George de Richelave, who had been with the Austrian military in the Great War, and he proceeded to put the stars through their paces. It took a long time for Aubrey to forget his British Army training and adapt to the Austrian methods, but eventually he managed to do it and earned the unqualified approval of the heel-clicking captain.

Movements of a different kind had been in evidence for *Never the Twain Shall Meet*, which was an inoffensive piece of nonsense with a South Seas setting, though, in fact, much of the filming had been done 'down coast' in an old sailing vessel called the *Moorea*. Before they had embarked, Aubrey reminded the chef that 'an actor acts on his stomach, and be sure not to go without plenty of meat.' On board with co-stars Leslie Howard and Conchita Montenegro, he had had a chance to show off his recently acquired technique for dancing South Seas style, with the gestures of the hands and the motion of the feet symbolising thoughts and needs.

For his encounter with *Tarzan the Ape Man* Aubrey had to be on 'African safari' in search of elephants' tusks. The story made the resulting film, with dialogue by Ivor Novello, probably the best of the Tarzan movies, and it is part of the childhood of nearly everyone over forty. Aubrey played James Parker, whose daughter (Maureen O'Sullivan) is carried off by Tarzan (Johnny Weissmuller), and after much 'impolite horse-play' and animal acting, and with 'Daddy' dead, she decides to stay with her 'noble savage' and his simian companions at the end of the picture. There are echoes of Conrad and Kipling in the tale, and such adventure yarns were dear to Aubrey's heart.

Aubrey had found a singular niche in the M.G.M. assembly line. So many of the pictures were built on a thin facade of sophisticated schmaltz, and Aubrey provided just the right kind of no-nonsense sincerity that brought a contrasting touch of realism. He was in *perpetuum mobile* in those early thirties, and though M.G.M. exploited his worth, for all their wealth, they occasionally 'loaned' him to other studios. He made *No More*

Orchids for Columbia – one wonders what Aubrey would have thought of 'His Crudeness' Harry Cohn as he strode through the Gower Street entrance of the studios and passed the plaque which read: 'In him the Strength of the Leader, the Flame of the Creator'; *They just had to get Married* for Universal; *Adorable* for Fox with a Paul Frank, Billy Wilder script; and for R.K.O. *Morning Glory*. In this Aubrey played the elderly actor Hedges, who takes under his wing the fledgling actress Eva Lovelace (Katherine Hepburn), and finally instils enough nous and confidence amongst the vulnerable precocity to make her a star. 'Beautiful, my dear, childishly beautiful,' says Hedges protectively of his protégé, who won an Academy Award for her performance. Their first meeting at a railway station had had comic possibilities:

Eva: You're English, aren't you?
Hedges: Yes, I am – or was. I've been here a long time.
Eva: They take me for English sometimes, but I could tell you were the real thing right off.

In an interview with Elsie Madison for the *L. A. Times Sunday Magazine*, which was published under the title 'Hollywood's Only Cockney', Aubrey gave his view of film production:

I don't know why the studios in Hollywood don't specialise. For instance, why doesn't one studio do all the historical plays, another the comedies, and so forth. Producers, actors, writers – nobody knows where he is. Now in England when I was young if you went with one theatre you decided right then and there just what type of thing you'd be. Over here, if one studio goes Shakespearean, then all the others vie with them for Shakespearean honours. If specialisation is good for one industry, why isn't it for another?

Aubrey was one of a number of stars who helped in the formation of the Screen Actors Guild in July of 1933, as a result of the demand by the studio bosses for a fifty per cent salary cut for all motion picture employees. The Depression had filtered through to the Pacific, cinema audiences had nearly halved, and almost a third of the 'screen houses' were closed. All the studios were affected, and even though M.G.M. was ahead of the rest, profits were at their lowest since the merger, and swingeing cuts were applied. Fear and animosity were rife in the industry, hurried conferences were organised, and a number of secret meetings were arranged. The livelihood of many was in danger, and to plan a protective Guild was a risky and courageous procedure. Aubrey had been busy early on in the cause of 'those less fortunate than ourselves', as he was to be later in the protracted dispute when he paraded on a picket line.

In the chapter 'He Had a Good Innings' from the biography of the cricket-loving 'Frankenstein', Boris Karloff, a founder member of the Guild, there is a vivid portrayal of Aubrey 'in impeccable snowy flannels, swooping about on the dance floor at the Hollywood Cricket Club (dances were held at the Hollywood Roosevelt Hotel), pausing, stage whispering through bristling white moustache to a fellow dancer: "My house tonight – not a word – park on another street – come in the back door ..." One, two, three, dip – and away.'

The story of the Hollywood Cricket Club and the game on the West Coast has been abridged in many newspaper and magazine articles, and often the screeds have not been devoid of exaggeration and embroidery, which is to be expected from a place where the exploitation of myth is part of its continued existence.

Aubrey did not start cricket in California, as is sometimes thought. The game had been played there for many years, and in fact in 1912 one Patrick J. Higgins is purported to have scored six centuries in one week. A British businessman, Ernie Wright, had done a lot of spadework with regard to making cricket a going concern, though with a lack of suitable pitches the twelve-team league had lapsed. Aubrey's arrival and active interest, however, created a resurgence that spread rapidly throughout the State. In no time he had approached the Provost of the University of California, Los Angeles and persuaded him to lend part of the campus at Westwood on specified days; the Hollywood Cricket Club was under way. In return, Boris Karloff and he would make themselves available to coach any students who wished to learn how to play. The white flannelled figures caused considerable amazement to onlookers, and, as David Niven recalls, 'car shunts on Sunset were not infrequent, as distracted drivers craned to see what was happening on the football and hockey field.'

At the inaugural meeting of the Hollywood Club, P. G. Wodehouse took the minutes and offered to help buy some of the equipment. Any remnants of social snobbery were stamped on quickly. Somebody objected to the membership of Karloff, the son of a diplomat in the Indian Civil Service, who was having to take jobs as a building labourer between film work, but the disapprobation was overruled immediately. The first members included many who were directly or indirectly connected with the movie industry: Claude King, Alan Mowbray, Stanley Mann, Herbert Marshall, Philip Merivale, Reginald Owen, Pat Somerset, and then a little later Melville Cooper, Fausto Acke, Douglas Walton, Frank Lawton, Nigel Bruce, H. B. Warner, who was caught playing without his cricket bat in his caravan during the filming of *King of Kings*; Laurence Olivier, who, it is reported, on his arrival in Hollywood when staying at the Château Marmont, found a note from Aubrey which read: 'There will be net practice tomorrow at 4 p.m. I trust I shall see you there'; and David Niven, who says that when 'that Grand Old Man asked you to play, you played.'

Aubrey was elected President of the Club, and the Vice-Presidents were Ronald Colman, Leon Errol, P. G. Wodehouse and George Arliss. Some of the membership was non-playing, or near non-playing. Olivier turned out perhaps once, and borrowed Karloff's cricket boots. He still thinks of Aubrey in his straw boater, and magenta, mauve and black striped blazer, with great affection. The filming of Daphne du Maurier's *Rebecca*, in which he starred opposite Joan Fontaine (who helped to sell programmes at charity matches during the War) with Aubrey as the magisterial Colonel Julyan, brings a fond memory. 'Ah, Mishish Danversh, won't you shit down?'

Niven was much more active. As a young actor trying to gain a foothold in the industry he had paid his $25 club subscription and, when not waylaid at Ciro's or by the Malibu Cocktail Circuit, was no mean performer on the field. In a game against Pasadena he had batted at number five in a side that had included three England Captains, two former and one current. Gubby Allen made the top score with seventy-seven, C. B. Fry hit twelve, Aubrey did not bat, and David scored thirteen. Incidentally, another England Captain visited Hollywood a few years later in 1939, when Archie MacLaren, whom Aubrey had first met on his debut for Lancashire in 1890, enjoyed a couple of days filming as a Crimean War veteran in *The Four Feathers*, in which Aubrey appeared with Ralph Richardson. Aubrey had secured the 'extra work' for Archie so that in between 'takes' they would get a good chance to have 'a decent natter'. There was, however, no opportunity to put on 'the whites'.

Within a very short time of the Hollywood games starting at U.C.L.A., cricket, which had lain dormant elsewhere in California, sprang to life. Clubs such as Venice, Santa Barbara, Ventura, San Diego and Montecito formed a fixture list, and Aubrey was the catalyst. The City Fathers eventually ceded some ground in Griffith Park after approaches had been made by the British Consulate, and after further persuasion from C. J. Williamson, a Park Commissioner at the Los Angeles Chamber of Commerce, a lover of the game and a member of the Hollywood Club. It came to be known as the C. Aubrey Smith Field; five cartloads of English grass seed was brought from across the water, a $30,000 pavilion was erected. At the dedication ceremony Aubrey's eyes were moist.

The Club became the social centre for the British Colony in Los Angeles, a focal point for expatriates who found security and satisfaction in recreating Rupert Brooke's lines in a foreign field. Aubrey saw it on many different levels. He, of course, enjoyed the sense of community, but in later years he realised its usefulness as a source of funds for help in war relief, and, naturally and foremost, he loved the cricket.

Though he had been in his late sixties when he first played in California, he continued to turn out regularly until 1940 when he took part in ten matches. After that appearances were more sporadic, though with the aid of a runner Aubrey went out to bat until the year of his death. In a letter to a friend in England dated August 28, 1943, in which he gave generous support to the East Molesey Club in their efforts to buy their ground, he wrote: 'I was persuaded to play again the other day ... and didn't I get a wigging when I got home for playing against Doctor's orders.' He was eighty and had been under the weather with 'a tired heart'.

During the Hollywood years he had scored sixty-one not out in a total of 106 against Murray Kinnell's XI (Kinnell helped discover Bette Davis for Warners), he had made forty-one not out against a South African side, which included a six and four fours, and in 1940, in his seventy-eighth year, he had reached double figures on five occasions. Apart from the usual sides playing for the Williamson Trophy, there were matches against East Indians, the Canadian Legion, and also the visiting Australians of 1932. Arthur Mailey, that clever exponent of leg spin and googly, had organised the tour which had begun in Canada and now was finishing in Los Angeles. In the games in Hollywood, the great Bradman scored fifty-two not out, eighteen not out, and eighty-three not out, to take his average to over one hundred for the entire trip.

In one of the games Aubrey was fielding at slip and dropped a catch, which was a rare event even in his seventieth year. The Don, who was at the non-striker's end, remembers Aubrey holding up the game and calling to Fred Loehndorf, who was his German chauffeur and 'man about the house', to bring him his spectacles. This was dutifully done, and the game resumed. Off the very next ball Aubrey dropped another catch. There was a stunned silence at the unparalleled event. Aubrey took off his spectacles and inspected them at arm's length. 'Egad, the clown's brought me my reading glasses!'

When batting, Aubrey had top scored with twenty-four, which contained a six and a four, before being caught by Vic Richardson off the wily Fleetwood-Smith, and while the Aussies remained in town he had kindly lent his Buick car to Bradman and his wife with Fred, who occasionally played for Hollywood, at the wheel accompanied by the Alsatian dog. In the course of tourists' stay, Paramount made a featurette called *Cricket Flickers*, highlighting the Aussies and Aubrey, and with Alan Kippax trying to teach Jack Oakie how to bat. There is an element of comedy in the 'short' as Oakie, typifying the American ignorance of cricket, tries vainly to adapt his ingrained baseball methods.

This 'cricket without tears' film is a reminder of the story – which may be apocryphal – of Hopalong Cassidy (William Boyd) turning out for one game as a replacement for a friend who had sprained his ankle, and, being unaware of the rules, handling the bat in baseball fashion rather like a policeman's truncheon. Having missed a couple of balls, he connected finally with a towering skier, whereupon he scampered off wildly on a circular tour, from point to cover to mid-off to mid-on to square-leg, until he finished helter-skelter plummeting arms akimbo into his own wicket. Aubrey provided the *coup de grâce*: 'Well, I declare!' What more was there to be said?

Aubrey was thought to be a stickler for discipline by some of the local players. Woe betide anybody who arrived for a game incorrectly dressed, or, even worse, was unpunctual. Eugene Walsh, who was a dentist from South Africa and one of the club's best players, remembers arriving ten minutes late at an arranged point from where Aubrey was to give him a lift. 'He gave me a thorough dressing-down. I was never late again,' says Walsh. The Canadian actor, Ted du Domaine once turned up two hours late for a match in San Francisco with a girl on each arm. Aubrey was not only furious but speechless. His main concern was that lackadaisical, slipshod, American habits, should not be allowed to infiltrate into the game and its ambience and thereby ruin it as a spectacle. It would have been all too easy to copy the trends of baseball; he fought to maintain the essential quality and decorum of cricket.

On a tour of British Columbia in 1936 he instructed all the team to be in bed by ten o'clock, in order to be fresh for the encounter with Vancouver on the morrow. Tommy Freebairn-Smith, who became the Hollywood secretary and also was a radio announcer, remembers that there were several attractive host team ladies in the offing, and with Errol Flynn and Frank Lawton in the side, Aubrey's command became wishful thinking. Nevertheless, next day 'Captain Blood' managed to score fourteen runs before being bowled, so he must have passed muster. In one of the games at Cowichan Bay an elderly gentleman came out to bat wearing a Carthusian tie. From second slip Aubrey directed: 'Spread the field chaps, spread the field!' 'The first ball nearly knocked the bat back into the wicket, the second whizzed past the off stump, and the third sent the middle stump flying,' says Freebairn-Smith. 'When we gathered around Aubrey for an explanation, he just stood scratching his head in puzzlement. "Senior to me at Charterhouse," said Aubrey, "used to knock 'em out of the ground." '

It was during this tour that 'Willie' Bruce excelled himself, both behind the stumps and in front. At one stage when batting he seemed to be getting carried away, and was aiming rash strokes at the wrong balls. 'Steady Willie, old chap, steady,' murmured Aubrey.

From all the team though there was a consensus of agreement for the words of Claude King at a celebratory dinner: 'Aubrey is the dearest soul I have ever met on God's green earth.'

Once, before a match in San Francisco, he was found in an excavated hole in the road holding a shovel and demonstrating to a group of Negro workmen how a cricket bat should be held, and in fact it was Aubrey who introduced the first black player into the Hollywood side.

He also paid for Desmond Roberts, who had played for Surrey Seconds, to journey to Hollywood, and managed to get him 'walk-on' parts in films. Roberts became one of the most prolific scorers for the club, and saved many a seemingly lost situation.

Hollywood C.C. now was a recognisable institution, and a decade or so later, in *The Loved One* by Evelyn Waugh, found not so much its doings described as the circumfused flavour of the time skilfully delineated, with the two Knights of the Realm, Sir Francis Hinsley and Sir Ambrose Abercrombie, in 'chivalric bond' rocking gently over a whisky and soda. Many were on the periphery of the cricket club's activities, even if not directly involved; for others the reverse was true: R. C. Sherriff, Anthony Bushell, Henry Stephenson, Ernest Torrance, Clive Brook, Basil Rathbone, Douglas Fairbanks Jnr., Arthur Wimperis and Clifford Severn, a homeopathic doctor who continued to bowl a straight line to the present author in the nets at Woodley Park in 1980 when he was a youthful ninety-one. Severn later formed his own club, Britamer, and had a handful of sons who played the game well. Actor Gilchrist Stuart was also a member of Hollywood, and so was

George Coulouris, whose main ambition was to have a travelling theatrical troupe that could double as a cricket team.

With the advent of war, Aubrey organised a number of games against and between docked battleships, all of them either in support of the Commando Benevolent Fund or some other War Relief Society, such as 'To Aid British Services'. At these sponsored matches stars would man the loudspeaker and distribute programmes. Helpers embraced the most attractive species of movieland: Greer Garson, Olivia de Havilland, Yvonne de Carlo, Gladys Cooper, Benita Hume, Evelyn Laye, Merle Oberon all had a turn at watching games and pulling crowds at Griffith Park or the Gilmore Stadium; nor did Cary Grant detract from the scenic beauty.

Aubrey's involvement with War Relief continued at home, and there were innumerable servicemen and British citizens who were given financial help. Not all of them deserved it. When his old colleague from the theatre, Brian Egerton, challenged him about spongers who never left his door empty handed, Aubrey said simply: 'Yes, I know, but when I remember all my good fortune – well, old son, good luck to 'em!'

Aubrey's 'good fortune' as he called it had manifested itself since he had settled in Beverly Hills. Initially he and his wife had rented properties, first in Horn Avenue just off Sunset Boulevard, and then at 1819 Coldwater Canyon. With the profusion of work however (Aubrey confided to Home Gordon that he was earning a steady £17,000 a year in the early thirties) they were able to purchase a charming little bungalow at 510 Rexford Drive and a larger Spanish house on Beverly Drive, both of which they leased out. In time the Beverly Drive property was swapped for another in exclusive Bel Air, and then this in turn was replaced by a house at 629 Rexford Drive, to which Aubrey and Tor moved just before he died. The house that the Smiths lived in themselves for the majority of their time in Los Angeles, and the one which is inextricably associated with Aubrey, was 'The Round Corner' at the top of Coldwater Canyon.

Aubrey had seen the location for the house at the junction with Mulholland Drive (incidentally, Isaac Hayes of *Shaft* renown lived there for a time in the last few years) while making *The Lives of a Bengal Lancer* for Paramount, which was released in 1935. He was smitten with the panoramic view, it being possible to see Santa Catalina Island on one side, and to the east the San Bernardino Mountains, which are snow-capped in winter. In the opposite direction was the forty-mile spread of the San Fernando Valley, and down at the bottom of the canyon was the Franklin Reservoir. The planning of the low rambling stucco house, and the landscaping of the garden, which involved mule teams led by Mexicans, was a major operation, and the Smiths were shocked when they learned that the architect to whom they had forwarded the money for building had not passed on any to his sub-contractors as he was in financial straits, and as a result had committed suicide. It meant, in effect, that a substantial portion had to be paid again.

Far less worrying had been Tor's endearing habit of assuming that while there remained a cheque in the cheque-book so there was money in the bank, and Aubrey seldom was short of surprises when checking the monthly accounts. Fundamentally both were happy in their new home and adopted land, and Aubrey once told a reporter: 'We love it for all it contains that *isn't* like England. We shouldn't really care to settle anywhere else now.'

Tor enjoyed gardening, where she had idiosyncratic assistance from the devoted Bavario, and Aubrey carpentering; being of a practical nature he used wooden posts and a clothes-line in devising a pulley to carry tools and materials up and down the steep slopes of the garden, which consisted in part of a bowling green before it took on a less trodden existence as a cornfield, a croquet lawn, an area for badminton, quoits, and 'clock' golf, and a babelish barnyard which harboured two goats, twenty rabbits, one sow, three piglets, and a clutch of chickens named after movie 'staresses'.

On the roof of the garage stood the weather vane with its famous three stumps, bat and ball, and through the War the Union Jack fluttered proudly on significant days. Fred Loehn-dorf's wife helped in the house, until eventually the Loehn-dorfs moved on and were replaced by a cheerful, companionable black American called Emery Jones. The Smiths entertained modestly rather than lavishly, preferring a dinner table for eight and a hand at Bridge afterwards. Dame May Whitty and her husband Ben Webster, the Hornblowers, Ethel

Barrymore, the Karloffs, and 'Willie' Bruce were regular visitors, and in conversation if ever anything denigrating was said about somebody Aubrey would ignore it, not wishing to know about the shortcomings of others. He was utterly guileless in this way, and obstinately refused to believe that people could be less than completely trustworthy; it was a constant worry to Tor that he was such an easy target for those on the 'make'. 'More people know Tom Fool than Tom Fool knows – where's my whisky?' he would say.

On one occasion his liking for the Scotch (he drank only moderately) nearly landed him in trouble. Aubrey had promoted the qualities of the libation so successfully amongst his guests, friends, and at one of his clubs, that he was persuaded to take out import licences to satisfy their growing demands:

'If I wasn't in the dog-house in Sacramento,' said Aubrey, 'I was over the fire in Washington. In the end I gave my paltry supply away, and retired to my livelihood as an actor. My deepest sympathy goes to the liquor and spirits dealers and importers of America. They must be a boon to unemployed secretaries and book-keepers. When you come down to it, I don't believe there is a drink in the world worth their trouble.'

The other time Aubrey took some 'stick' was when the *Los Angeles Examiner* ran a column pillorying 'British bums' and 'Communists', such as David Niven, Ronald Colman, C. Aubrey Smith, Basil Rathbone and Cedric Hardwicke. Apparently, the five actors had unsuspectingly contributed to a Communist Front Organisation when a *chicano* had wandered round the set with a collecting box, mumbling incoherently about starving Mexican lettuce pickers.

As far as his clubs were concerned, the Garrick, the Green Room, the Sports and Camera in London, the Players in New York, and the Hollywood Athletic, and the Masquers in Los Angeles, Aubrey used them as a grapevine to hear of the latest happenings and aired projects in the 'business'. Essentially he was too domesticated to be an archetypal 'club man', and his appearances though welcome were irregular.

'Business' for Aubrey had been good; the milch cow continued to produce, and if the flow was less torrential than in those first few summers, the quality of his work was unimpaired by advancing years. He had struck back with *Bulldog*

Drummond for United Artists in 1934, and just before that as the Duke of Wellington befriended the brilliant Nathan Mayer in *The House of Rothschild* for the same company. As Aage, personal guard to *Queen Christina*, he had stood out from the rest of the entourage surrounding Greta Garbo. As it happened the Swedish Goddess lived close to the Smiths in Beverly Hills, and would sometimes pop in to relax in that aura of protective calm away from the apple-polishy socialising of the immediate vicinity. With Garbo's permission, Aubrey took his daughter Honor on to the set to watch her filming, which was an almost unheard of privilege at any time during her career. It was not the only time that Aubrey watched Garbo in action, and the distinguished director George Cukor remembers that in the shooting of one scene Garbo started to feel *louche* and awkward, went up to Aubrey, flung her arms round his neck, smiled and said: 'Dearest Aubrey, you *do* understand, don't you?'

In '34, he filmed with another legendary lady when he played Prince August with Marlene Dietrich as Catherine II in *The Scarlet Empress*. The next year, and ten films later, he took the part of Pitt the Elder in *Clive of India*, which provided a vehicle for one of Ronald Colman's finest performances, and then strolled along to the Paramount lot for *The Crusades*, which was a Cecil B. de Mille production under the auspices of the studio chief who was destined to become the cinema's centenarian, Adolph Zukor. Aubrey had worked for de Mille before as Mark Antony's friend Enobarbus in *Cleopatra*, and the two films were set in roughly the same part of the globe. The dialogue aped de Mille's grandiloquence: 'Stop blasphemer! I go, but I will come again, and with me shall come the great Crusades!' cried Aubrey, as the Hermit, being given the heave-ho by Saladin who has just made a spectacular entrance with his cortège.

After an outing in *China Seas* with Clark Gable, Jean Harlow, Rosalind Russell and Wallace Beery, Aubrey reverted to type as the Earl of Dorincourt in *Little Lord Fauntleroy*. Naomi Jacob wrote: 'The American actors may have been good, but Aubrey made them all look - nothing. He didn't walk, he stalked into the room. He handed his hat to the footman without ever looking at him - it was evident that he *expected* someone to be there to take it.'

The Screen Actors' Guild of America voted Aubrey's Dorincourt a tie with William Powell's Ziegfeld as the best performance of the month. David O. Selznick, the producer of *Fauntleroy* and second to none in his regard for the Grand Old Man, immediately gave him a five-year contract, which was a vindication for Aubrey's decision to turn down Louis B. Mayer's offer of a further spell at M.G.M. at a reduced rate. 'You're no younger than when you started,' had been the arch-schemer's intelligent appraisal.

Aubrey was given a substantial part in Selznick's next picture *The Garden of Allah*, and in order to play Father Roubier, the desert priest, he was required to spend three weeks on location in the fearsome heat of arid Arizona. The sun shone relentlessly, and at noon the temperature regularly registered 120 degrees plus. Charles Boyer was taking seven or eight showers a day, and apparently Marlene Dietrich fainted three times. Aubrey sat in his one-roomed wooden hut imperturbably puffing on his pipe.

Irving Thalberg, who had been dubbed 'the boy wonder' at M.G.M., was next in line for Aubrey's services, and few who have seen *Romeo and Juliet* will forget Lord Capulet's dramatic exit through the cathedral door with the citizens crying: 'Down with the Capulets, down with the Montagues'. Norma Shearer, Leslie Howard, John Barrymore and Basil Rathbone headed a strong cast.

'I seem condemned to be a colonel sahib or a padre these days,' said Aubrey half ruefully, 'yet I don't entirely dislike the type.' He had just been cast as the seemingly hard-hearted soldier grandfather of the juvenile darling of cinema-goers, little Shirley Temple in *Wee Willie Winkie*. 'Hollywood takes the most astonishing liberties, and does the most astounding things, but seems to get away with it. As a lover of Rudyard Kipling, I was horrified at the changes they made in the story. The film is no more like Rudyard Kipling's masterpiece than it is like *Alice in Wonderland*. I went to the première in fear and trembling and, much to my surprise, thoroughly enjoyed the picture. It is excellent entertainment, and Shirley Temple surpasses herself.'

Anyone who sees David O. Selznick's 1937 version of *The*

Prisoner of Zenda might be excused for thinking that the British Colony had manufactured a take-over bid. Ronald Colman, Madeleine Carroll, Raymond Massey, David Niven and, of course, Aubrey, dominate the picture. Mary Astor and Douglas Fairbanks Junior must have felt very lonely in their own land, and indeed after the public revelations from *Dear Diary* Miss Astor must have felt grateful to Aubrey, one of the few to treat her as if nothing had happened.

Filming of *The Prisoner of Zenda* started in the February with a scene which called for Colman to shake hands with himself. James Wong Howe, the cinematographer, had devised a simple but clever optical illusion which worked extremely well. In between takes Aubrey would sit on a chair reading *The Times* with the help of an eye-glass, and with his ear trumpet turned off. As he grew older he became increasingly deaf and relied on an assistant to warn him when he was to be needed. This was never a problem, because from prop boy to production manager he commanded great respect and affection. Always he arrived on set at the scheduled time, was line perfect, and was known to treat everybody with the same degree of courtesy. Aubrey never would read the local 'rags', and the reason he gave was that he did not wish to wade through the intimacies of somebody's pigeon-holes, or the intricacies of somebody else's divorce to find information of international importance. Consequently, often he was reading news that was two weeks stale. 'Good God!' The sudden explosion from the chair startled everyone. 'You know that blighter Hitler has attacked the Sudetenland!'

Douglas Fairbanks, who was cast as Rupert of Hentzau, recalls Raymond Massey, playing Black Michael, pacing up and down in an agitated fashion during a break in filming. Eventually Massey tapped Aubrey on the shoulder. 'Aubrey,' he said concernedly, 'I'm very worried about this part. I can't get the motivation – the reasoning behind this character – you must help me.' Aubrey glanced up with a reassuring smile. 'My dear Raymond, during my time I've played every part in *The Prisoner of Zenda* with the exception of Princess Flavia. I've *always* had trouble with Black Michael ...'

One day Aubrey looked slightly downcast. 'Is anything the matter, sir?' asked David Niven, who automatically called

Aubrey 'sir' as a mark of respect, even though as Fritz von Tarlenheim he was required to do so when addressing Colonel Zapt in the kingdom of Ruritania.

'Well, Davy boy, I'm worried about these cuts they're making in the dear old play, you know.'

'What have they cut out, sir?'

'The best line in the piece, you know.'

'What's that, sir?'

'Well, when I say to Rudolf "Englishman, you are the finest Elphberg of them all". It's been taken out, Davy boy, it's been taken out, and that's dreadful.'

'Davy boy' had a quick word with David O., the producer, who said immediately 'Oh, we must put it back in again,' and then David O. had a quicker word with John Cromwell, the director, and all seemed to be well. The line was reinstated, but with the proliferation of directors who arrived to tighten the tempo towards the end of filming, somehow once more it vanished into thin air.

'Oh, by heaven, Davy boy, ruining the dear old play, you know.'

The line continued to lead a chequered existence, *in* one day, *out* the following, *in* again, *out* again, until it started to assume a proportion that demanded a chapter all to itself.

Finally filming finished, and at last the count *the* line had been out. Aubrey was dismayed, to say the least, and it seemed certain that posterity never would have the chance to find out just how *fine* an Englishman could be. And then suddenly there was a recall on to the set for Rudolf, Fritz and Colonel Zapt. The last scene had to be retaken. They rode on horses to the edge of the forest.

Fritz: Goodbye Rudolf, we'll meet again?
Rudolf: Goodbye Fritz – Goodbye Colonel.
                              Pause
Colonel Zapt: Goodbye Englishman, you are the finest Elphberg of them all …

And so it ended, happily ever after.

Aubrey now ventured into deep water. *The Hurricane* pounding the shores of a picturesque Polynesian atoll dished out severe physical punishment, and Aubrey in his rôle as the priest, Father Paul, had to stand and take it for five weeks. He did manage one morning off, though, while a doctor asked him to take off his shirt. While playing cricket for Hollywood at San Diego on a Sunday afternoon he had had two ribs fractured when attempting to cover drive a fiery fast bowler. Raymond Massey, who was cast as De Laage the implacable governor of Manakoora, reports that the director, Jack Ford, told Aubrey jokingly that 'he was not responsible for youngsters going off and engaging in dangerous sports while working on one of his routine pictures.' Aubrey was more than a little embarrassed.

Mary Astor and Dorothy Lamour were also in the film, which was shot in Samuel Goldwyn's back lot across the way from the Gas Company in Formosa Street. The effects of the terrifying hundred mile an hour gales produced by wind machines, and the tanks holding 150,000 gallons of water, created a vividly realistic drowning of Father Paul as he stood in his half-submerged, doomed church, comforting his flock of South Sea islanders, with gigantic waves breaking down the walls of the edifice. Aubrey received much praise and publicity for his performance, and gave his views to the weekly *Picturegoer*:

> In the early days of the films, character players were just necessary evils. The lovely heroine had to have a crabbed old father or a scheming uncle. There must, perforce, be mothers, grandmothers, middle-aged villains, and kindly old men.
>
> Today, the character player stands on his own merits, is given rôles of outstanding, sometimes stellar, importance. Youth and beauty will, of course, always be dominant in the cinema, where visual appeal counts for so much. One could scarcely expect, for example, the public to be as interested in Father Paul, the aged priest of *The Hurricane*, as in Terangi and Marama, the vital native youths played by Jon Hall and Dorothy Lamour. But Father Paul is a powerful character, essential to the plot structure. He is, bless him, typical of all that an actor who has spent more than 40 years with the theatre could wish for.

And Aubrey it was who had done so much to further the position of the character actor.

For *Four Men and a Prayer* Aubrey teamed up once again with David Niven, though as Aubrey played the cashiered Colonel Leigh, who is victimised by a foul conspiracy and then is murdered early on, he was not one of the four 'gents'. That privilege fell to William Henry, Richard Green, George Sanders and David, who took the rôles of a student, an attaché, a rising barrister, and a R.A.F. Officer – and Loretta Young was the Prayer!

In the middle of one 'take' when George Sanders as the barrister was 'acting up a storm', getting quite carried away with the part and almost in tears, David Niven as Chris came in with his best 'flying voice' bang on cue. Unfortunately it had the effect of destroying a dramatic and potent pause at the end of the oration, and Jack Ford, who was directing, lost his 'Irish' and gave David 'the wigging of his life' in front of the assembled cast and cameramen. Aubrey immediately took the irate director to one side and reminded him in no uncertain terms that Niven was only a boy without much experience, and that he (Ford) should know better than to behave like that. Ford, considerably abashed, humbly agreed, and subsequently made a huge effort to be extraordinarily nice to David whenever their paths crossed.

Once again Aubrey took to the high seas, though this time it was 'for real'. He returned to England to see the Test Matches against the Aussies, to film *Sixty Glorious Years* with Anna Neagle for Alexander Korda and, appropriately, to be made a Commander of the British Empire as well. For the investiture at Buckingham Palace he donned knee-breeches, and made an imposing figure for the many photographers who gathered in the courtyard to take his picture.

It had been approximately two years since he had last journeyed to his native soil, and he appreciated the chance offered to relax and enjoy the social life of an ocean liner. A Cunard White Star first-class passenger list of R.M.S. *Berengaria* from around that period makes fascinating reading: Mr Charles Boyer, Mr Joseph P. Kennedy, Mrs Kennedy, Mr Jack Kennedy, Mr Ray Noble, Miss Merle Oberon, and Mr

C. Aubrey Smith and Manservant.

But when it came to the home country Aubrey was a trifle disenchanted, as is obvious from an interview with the writer W. J. Makin:

I've had some magnificent times in England. I loved it. But I'm speaking in the past tense. I find the England of today is not the England I loved yesterday. I went to search for the country and the people I loved. One of the first things I did was to sit in the pavilion at Lord's. I had thought of that thrilling moment during years of exile out here. And then, on that summer's day at Lord's, came the realisation. Bitter.

The flannel-clad figures on the pitch were as skilful as ever, and playing cricket as only Englishmen can play it. But I missed the familiar characters, and the deep affection that would come to them in quiet grunts and 'Well-played, sir' from the spectators. I missed, too, the old familiar faces in the pavilion. I found myself a stranger sitting amongst strangers.

That evening I went to my old club. There, a similar disappointment awaited me. All the old friends had gone. New faces, new members. Only the wine-steward remembered me. Why do wine-stewards live to such a fruity old age?

In desperation I bought a car and set off with my wife to motor through the green heart of England. We crossed the Cotswolds and entered the Wye Valley. But the scenery was blurred in wetness. Rain and more rain. It became worse as we entered Wales. I even experienced an almost-forgotten twinge of rheumatism. In sheer despair, we turned back towards London.

I went in search of my home village. I recalled its superb situation, on a hill in Middlesex with the spread of Bucks in the distance. Another tragedy awaited me. Gone was the old Tudor house with its beautiful weathered brick and beams. Gone the stream that crossed the middle of the lane, and was a romantic spot for all boys. Instead, there was a block of newly built cheap cottages. The whole beauty of the place had been spoiled. An arterial road straddled in the distance, with more cheap houses flanking it. They call it ribbon development, eh? Well, I hate it. It's spoiled the old countryside. I went back to London and booked my passage to California. I wasn't sorry to leave.

Aubrey nuzzled the neck of Bodor his Great Dane (a gift from Boris Karloff. The dog's name came from an amalgam of Boris and his wife Dorothy), and pulled ruminatively on his pipe.

With *Kidnapped* out of the way, and then a sojourn in Universal Studios in *East Side of Heaven, The Sun Never Sets* and *The Under-Pup*, Aubrey proceeded to fulfil his two-film agreement with Korda in *The Four Feathers*, which had screenplay by R. C. Sherriff and featured John Clements, Ralph Richardson and June Duprez. The colour setting was by Vincent Korda, and the direction by Zoltan Korda, so there was no doubt for which production company the actors were working.

The story of *The Four Feathers*, which is too well known to need much elucidation, is set in the Sudan of 1885, and follows the capture of Khartoum by the rebellious Dervishes, and the killing of General Gordon. Aubrey took the part of General Burroughs, and some of the dialogue is a hilarious but priceless reminder of a bygone age:

General Burroughs raises his glass in a toast
with Harry Faversham and Doctor Sutton

Burroughs: The Crimea by jove! War was war in those days, and men were men. No room for weaklings. Now here (*dips his finger into a glass of wine, and draws a line across the table*) these nuts were the Russians, guns, guns, guns (*places pineapples on table*). On the right the British Infantry, the thin red line, and here was I, at the head of the old 68th. One of my subalterns came to me shaking, absolutely shaking. I said, what's wrong Travers? He said, I'm afraid to face those guns sir. I said, would you rather face me! Hm. He took one look at my face and off he went. Ten minutes later he was shot to pieces at the head of his men. As a soldier should be eh?

(*Fear not, readers, it doesn't end there.*)

Burroughs: Do you remember Wilmington?
General Faversham: Wilmington?
Burroughs: Fine old service family. Father killed at Inkermann,
   grandfather blown up under Nelson, an uncle scalped by
   Indians – oh, splendid record, splendid.
Faversham: What happened?
Burroughs: Well, the General ordered him to gallop through
   the front lines with a message. Paralysed with funk.
   Couldn't move. General sent his adjutant, killed before he'd
   gone 50 yards. Sent his A.D.C. – head blown off. Then he
   went through with the message himself – lost his arm,
   ruined his cricket.

The famous literary egocentric James Agate went to the
première of *The Four Feathers*, and it brought back memories
of an incident at the St Martin's Theatre on the first night of *A
Bill of Divorcement*. After the first act Agate felt a tap on his
shoulder and a voice said: 'Tell me, sir, would that be Mr
Aubrey Smith?' 'It would,' was Agate's reply. The middle-aged
interlocutor went on: 'I was at Cambridge with him, and he
batted like that.'
   Coincidentally in the next year, 1940, and after a return to
the M.G.M. fold in the musical *Balalaika*, Aubrey was to
renew his interest in *A Bill of Divorcement*, this time for David
Selznick, and with Adolphe Menjou, Maureen O'Hara and
Dame May Whitty helping in the action.
   In the winter of 1941 Aubrey faced an audience instead of a
camera. He had been delighted to accept an invitation to go
back to Broadway and tread the boards again with his friend
and partner of so many years ago, Grace George. In a way it
was an exercise in Darby and Joanship, though the comedy
Spring Again by Isabel Leighton and Bertram Bloch at Henry
Miller's Theatre received glowing notices. Richard Watts
Junior's review in the *New York Herald Tribune* was typical:

   It is a rare delight to have Mr Smith back in the theater,
   and he is altogether wonderful in his performance, even if it
   is not easy to think of him as the son of an American general
   of Civil War days. Having been for so long the favourite
   British commander in chief of us all, he has become so

monumental a figure that it is almost impossible to think of him as the offspring of a great soldier, and not that great soldier himself. Indeed, that monumental quality is so impressive that it is difficult to think of him as a son of anyone save possibly of some ancient chieftain of Britain who had warred against Julius Caesar. But it would be a delight and a comfort to see him, no matter what he happened to be playing.

'This is my first playing here since *The Bachelor Father*,' Aubrey told reporters, 'and I love it! I've had fifty years of the stage and the screen, but I want a lot more. When I'm an even hundred years old I'll retire, but not before. Retire and go back to cricket. And maybe to Johannesburg.'

Acting every evening with Grace George revived memories of their long tour together in *A Woman's Way*. It gave Aubrey his first view of the Pacific. 'It was the most beautiful thing I've ever seen. It was orange and purple. There was a lot of kelp that day, and that peculiar purple colour that no other water ever has.' As a postscript to *Spring Again* it is interesting to discover that taking the role of a Western Union Boy was twenty-five-year-old Issur Danielovich Demsky, alias Kirk Douglas.

Aubrey was soon to embark on a lengthy stage tour around the States and Canada in *Old English*, and this gave him an opportunity to raise funds for the war effort by selling his signature for ten cents a time. In a remarkably short spell he had collected several thousand dollars. This was only one of several activities specifically aimed at helping the Forces.

Radio was another outlet – Forces broadcasting with Gracie Allen, George Burns and others, and also the organising of live concerts for the Navy. In one of these radio shows Aubrey teamed up with 'Willie' Bruce and Sir Cedric Hardwicke as a vocal trio to sing *Three Little Fishes*, and it is obvious from the recording who is getting the greatest fun out of the performance. After the war was over Aubrey appeared in a B.B.C. programme that was devoted to those with the surname 'Smith', and in 1947 he was welcomed on to *Flotsam's Follies* on the old Home Service, and the following verses were heard over the air:

SIR AUBREY

We've had a fine ambassador in Hollywood for years;
   A legend he's become, but not a myth;
      Now he's paying us a visit;
      Any need to say who is it?'
No. Not any need; you're right, it's Aubrey Smith.

And they don't come any better than Sir Aubrey,
   With the beetling eyebrows everybody knows;
      Eyebrows said to beetle more
      Than eyebrows ever did before,
   Part and parcel of his prepossessing pose;
      With those clefts in chin and cheek,
      And that aristocratic beak,
And that healthy tan that's *not* bucolic strawberry,
      And that figure tall and nifty
      Coveted by men of fifty,-
Oh, they don't come any better than Sir Aubrey.

Fieldmarshals, bishops, admirals, explorers and M.P.'s
   Any type who's got unsullied kin and kith-
      Are his cup of tea; and few sirs
      Of the Hollywood producers
   Ever hesitate; they send for Aubrey Smith
For they don't come any better than Sir Aubrey,

   If his part's the Earl of Something, well, he's *it*;
      Most occasions, by a fluke, he's
      Much more ducal than a Duke is,-
   He can register, what's more, in any 'bit';
      When it comes to being 'pukka',
      Looking fresh after a 'chukka',
Why they don't come any better than Sir Aubrey.

No, they don't come any better than Sir Aubrey;
   California claimed him many years ago;
      At first he couldn't stick it,
      So he got them playing cricket;
   Having been a county player, as you know;
      By the Yanks he's rated 'super',
      And he's still a grand old trouper,
And an enemy of all that's slack and tawdry,

So it's not surprising, is it?
That we're glad to have him visit,
For they don't come any better than Sir Aubrey.

After his Indian Summer on the stage in the early forties, Aubrey returned to Hollywood and the film lots. He was unequivocal in his attitude towards the two mediums.

'I've seen the screen overshadow the stage in my time,' he told Makin, 'yet I cannot see the stage dying. The two mediums should and will work together for their mutual advantage. There is no dramatic school equal to the stage. Acting technique must have a solid foundation. That foundation can best be acquired in the theatre. The screen, in turn, can provide new blood for the stage.'

In *Flesh and Fantasy* in 1943 Aubrey displayed facets of his own acting technique and characterisation that transcended and made an exception (as was mentioned much earlier) of any typecast with which he was apt to be put. In ecclesiastical rôles (in this film he played the Very Reverend Dean of Norwalk, or possibly of Chichester, depending on whether you believe the sound track or the captions) Aubrey seemed to adopt a subtle range of Christian gentleness and meekness that is not only compelling, but completely captivating, and it is a side that should have been exploited far more. The film had a premonitory plot and displayed three contrasting views of the future. Dame May Whitty died more or less naturally, whereas Aubrey, down in the wine cellar fetching the port, narrowly escaped a clout on the 'crust' from a mallet wielded by the Latinate, Edward G. Robinson.

The White Cliffs of Dover was a sentimental, patriotic 'hands across the sea' drama, which drew an enormous Miniver public both sides of the Atlantic. During the shooting there was a tense moment when the director, Clarence Brown, sent the dancing instructor across to Aubrey to teach him how to waltz with Irene Dunne. 'Coach me in the waltz, miss,' he said indignantly. 'You spend your time with the jitterbugs. I'll take care of Miss Dunne.' Whereupon he took his co-star in his arms and nimbly one, two, three'd around the set.

For another scene Aubrey was required to run up and down stairs, and Brown worriedly whispered to his crew: 'Remember,

boys, a "take" first time, we have an old man to think about.'
Aubrey was in earshot. 'Old man, indeed! Old boy!' he roared.
'We'll see about that,' and he proceeded to scamper up and
down the staircase twice, in double quick time.

On his eightieth birthday his friends had arranged a dinner
in his honour at Chasen's in Beverly Hills. Celery en Branche,
Mission Ripe Olives and Vermicelli Al'novo fended off hunger
pangs, and Prime Ribs of Beef au Jus made sure that nobody
needed to stop at a takeaway on the way home. The British
Colony were there in force: Ronald Colman, 'Willie' Bruce,
Cedric Hardwicke, Philip Merivale, Basil Rathbone, Halliwell
Hobbes, Boris Karloff, Brian Aherne, John Cromwell, Herbert
Marshall, Ivan Simpson, who sculpted a bust of Aubrey to
stand beneath the Whistler etchings in his study, novelist
James Hilton, and playwright Arthur Wimperis who wrote
some verses for the occasion:

TO C. A. S.

A Gentleman was born today
Whose advent caused but little stir;
The Times had only this to say:
'To Mrs Smith – a cricketer.'

A cricketer of parts, God wot!
Some strokes he had that shocked the Highbrows,
But woe to him who risked a shot
Where Smith lay ambushed in his eyebrows!

A tower of strength when things were tough,
A bag of tricks on grass or matting,
He bowled that round-the-corner stuff
That played Old Harry with the batting.

From Fenner's to the Village Green,
With any side on any wicket,
The Stage, the Stock Exchange, the Screen,
What Aubrey played was always cricket.

So lift a brimming glass herewith,
For here tonight we think it proper
To drink a toast to Aubrey Smith,
The Bowler whom we found a Topper.

If whom the world can truly say,
'*A Gentleman* was born today.

In June of '44 the 'born Gentleman' was knighted by King George VI. Aubrey was concerned that he might not be able to rise quickly after being dubbed, but assistance was at hand, and all was well. The King remembered attending the Command Performance at which Aubrey had played over thirty years before, and asked questions about his manufactured 'stage fall' on that occasion. Aubrey in turn told the King of the time when his grandfather John Clode, Mayor of Windsor, had been knighted by Queen Victoria.

A month later the British United Services Club of Los Angeles paid homage to the new Knight and his Lady at the Masquers Club in Hollywood, and Gracie Fields topped the bill. There was general rejoicing that at last proper recognition had arrived for the Grand Old Man of Hollywood. Actor Brian Egerton recalled the words of the British Consul, who when newly appointed to Los Angeles heard that he was in for a tough time. 'Well,' he had said, 'I have had no difficulty or trouble. Aubrey has made it all plain sailing – he's about the best Ambassador we could wish to have.'

The sentiments were shared in London, and Home Gordon puts forward an interesting sidelight: 'At the Garrick it was curious how his innate unobtrusiveness always seemed to dominate the assertive obviousness of sundry other members. As an old cricketer said to me: "Round the Corner" can only be described as Dearly Beloved.'

Aubrey carried on working as hard as ever, and starred in two *Scotland Yard* films for Republic, and in the second he played Sir James Collison, curator of the British National Art Gallery, who has to withstand the wiles of Carl Hoffmeyer, an unscrupulous art devotee, played by Erich Von Stroheim. He remained *Unconquered* in Hollywood, which was a publicity headline promoting Cecil B. de Mille's latest epic. In his autobiography, de Mille wrote: 'With all due respect for the performances of Gary Cooper, Paulette Goddard, Howard da Silva, Boris Karloff, Cecil Kellaway and Ward Bond, my two heroes in *Unconquered* were Sir C. Aubrey Smith and Robert Baughman. Sir Aubrey, well past eighty years of age, would come on set each morning with his lines letter perfect, giving the director a joy which much younger players, alas, sometimes deny him.'

At the age of eighty-three Aubrey signed another contract with Sir Alexander Korda, and when celebrating his golden wedding anniversary in the August of that year, 1946, he told interviewers: 'Any man can stay married 50 years if he allows himself to be henpecked!' Beneath his bushy eyebrows flashed a wink. He still was busy arranging for new cricketing gear to be sent across the Atlantic for the Hollywood Club and also the other elevens who played on the four grounds he had helped acquire for the game, and whenever he visited England he placed an order for the necessary items that could not be found in Sam Goldwyn's 'outpost of civilization'.

In 1947 Aubrey came once more to his 'sceptred isle'. It was a decade or so since 'young Compton' had tweaked his left-armers to him in the nets at Lord's for a 'five bob' tip, but he lost no time in finding his old cricket ground on the South Coast. As Aubrey entered through the gates from Eaton Road, a county game was in progress for James Langridge's benefit. Aubrey appeared lost, uncertain, and wandered on to the grass in front of the pavilion. It was many years since he had last been there. Suddenly he saw the Committee Room, and started to walk towards it, and the watching crowd, who by this time had recognised him, burst into a spontaneous round of applause. The players were distracted, puzzled, nothing much was happening out on the field, but when they realised the reason for the public reaction they responded as well.

Aubrey also revisited Cambridge. He saw the Master of St John's and went to his old room: it was still the same but somehow different.

He wandered along to Buttress's, the outfitters with whom he had dealt when he was 'up', and bought twelve ties for the Club and socks for himself, and then he lunched at the University Arms, and signed autographs for the curious clientele. He had tea at the Hawks Club, and began to reminisce. He remembered a 'rag' he had played against a man called Barrett. Barrett used to give lavish breakfast parties in College, and so one day Aubrey and a friend invited about thirty people to a morning junket at Barrett's room. When they arrived they found nothing but half a cold sausage, a pint of beer, and, of course, the hapless occupant, who was summarily dispatched into a bath of cold water.

Aubrey also had his portrait painted, as a result of a commission by the Green Room Club to a fellow member, the distinguished artist, John Gilroy. Gilroy, who had had several Royal 'sitters', found Aubrey a memorable subject, with the aquiline profile, large knobbly hands (revealing many clashes with inflexible 'leather'), and, above all, powerful character, easy to draw.

Some of the sittings took place at 'Great Fosters' in Egham, where Aubrey and his wife were staying during the filming of *An Ideal Husband*, which was distributed by British Lion for 20th Century Fox. Alex Korda directed Paulette Goddard, Michael Wilding, Hugh Williams, Diana Wynyard and Aubrey in the adaptation of the play by Oscar Wilde, and the film critics felt that 'it was a pleasure to see Lord Caversham played by Sir Aubrey Smith with customary charm and distinction.'

The Earl of Caversham: Warmest congratulations, Robert – I've just left the Prime Minister. You're to have the vacant seat in the Cabinet.
Sir Robert Chiltern: A seat in the Cabinet?
Caversham: Certainly. And you well deserve it. You've got what we need so much nowadays in political life. High character, high moral tone, high principles ...
Chiltern: I cannot accept this offer, Lord Caversham. I have to decline it.
Caversham: You'd decline it?
Chiltern: It's my intention to retire at once from public life.
Caversham: Decline a seat in the Cabinet, and retire from public life? I've never heard of such nonsense in the whole course of my existence ...

And nor would Aubrey ever have retired from public life. He rejected an offer to stay in England for *Bonnie Prince Charlie* with David Niven, as it would have meant facing the rigours of a British winter, and so he went back to where he began in the 'talking picture' world, at M.G.M. in Hollywood for *Little Women* with June Allyson, Peter Lawford, Janet

Leigh, Elizabeth Taylor and Mary Astor. When that was completed, he was asked to play the rôle that he said he wanted to play more than any he had ever attempted, 'Old Jolyon' in *The Forsyte Saga*, and on Tuesday, 21st of December 1948 he was due to report at the studio for wardrobe tests.

A few days before, however, Aubrey was forced to take to his bed with a cold, and double pneumonia developed on the Friday. Even though his condition was serious it was not considered critical, but near midnight on the following Sunday he suffered a setback, became worse, and at 12.25 a.m. on Monday, 20th of December, he died.

He always had been 'chesty', easily susceptible to a chill, though it is ironic to remember that at the age of thirty-three doctors had given him six months to live unless he refrained from smoking. He did – for four months.

In his long career Aubrey had played many parts, on field, stage and set as well as elsewhere. The figures alone are hard to digest, because apart from a very approximately estimated three and a half thousand runs and five and a half hundred wickets in front line cricket, from his days at Cambridge he appeared in almost one hundred stage plays, and in over one hundred films. But the figures are not the man, nor had they ever been. When Fritz von Tarlenheim in *The Prisoner of Zenda* said to Rudolf Rassendyll 'Heaven doesn't always make the right men Kings,' by his side was Colonel Zapt. He could have been addressing Aubrey, though in fact the 'Grand Old Man' always had been a King, and rightfully so.

Nine months later, Sir Aubrey's ashes were buried in St Leonard's Churchyard, Hove, but a week after his death a Memorial Service was held at All Saints' Episcopal Church, Beverly Hills. The British Colony were there *en masse*, the service was conducted by the Rev. J. Herbert Smith, and Douglas Fairbanks Junior read a specially composed tribute by the author of *Lost Horizon*, James Hilton:

Eighty-five years ago there was born in England a man whom destiny held in special favour. He was to achieve much fame in his own chosen profession, he was to win private happiness and popular esteem, he was to serve his country in peace as well as war and to receive its high and deserved honour; he was to find one place, in his own heart, for England and America, and to be loved equally in both. And finally he was to reach a great age and to die surrounded by friends. There could be no nobler pattern for any man's life, and it was that of Charles Aubrey Smith.

Aubrey's years, because they were so many, take us far into the past. When he was a small boy there were a few people still living who had seen George Washington and many who had fought at Waterloo. The Franco-Prussian War had just ended when Aubrey went to Charterhouse, and when later he entered St John's College, Cambridge, Disraeli was the great name and the Queen was not so very old. It was at Charterhouse and Cambridge that Aubrey discovered himself both as an actor and a cricketer, and from then onwards the stage and the green fields, the footlights and the summer sunshine, were his forever. A young dramatic critic named Bernard Shaw praised his acting, and an elderly cricketer named W. G. Grace chose 'Round the Corner Smith' to bowl for his team. It was all a virile blend of work that was pleasure, and pleasure that meant hard and healthy activity.

And so the years went by, and the old Queen died, and presently there came into existence the new art of the cinema that could magnify both fames and faces as never before. Aubrey, by this time married and with a family, was already well-known on the English stage, but after the first world war, in which he served as a second lieutenant, he travelled widely in America and gradually came to settle where films were being made. It was the beginning, in his sixties, of a new career.

This brings us to the heart of the matter – which was and always will be, a man's real self and character. There ran in Aubrey's blood a stream direct from Chaucer's and Shakespeare's England, sweet as an English apple, strong and straight and humorous and full of the generous sportsmanship that has made the very word cricket come to mean so much more than just a word. Every friend of Aubrey's knew and loved these qualities in him, and by the strange miracle of the camera they came through to the millions who knew him only by sight. And thus began the unique phase of

Aubrey's life. He became very modestly (and hardly himself realising it) in some sense an Ambassador of and between the two countries he loved. He *was* England, to a great many – perhaps an older England, but an England rich in dignity, graciousness and good will. Certainly no one could ever have known him, either in life or on the screen, without liking England better afterwards, and no one ever did more, without words or preachment, to bring the English and American spirit closer to the same heartbeat of humanity. That unforgettable face, those strong sensitive features, became somehow a symbol of character in a world in danger of losing it, and when towards the end the King made him a knight, it was the fitting thing – because that mingling of strength and gentleness which is the true knightly essence, had been Aubrey's all along.

And so in the fullness of time this long rich valiant happy life came to an end, and it is clear that we are gathered here today not for distress or to mourn, but rather to take pride that we knew such a man, that we lived part of our lives with his, and that the two countries he most loved are our own. The world is not lost while such men are remembered, because their way of life is of immortal Christian quality – true, faithful, lovable – 'with malice towards none, with charity for all'. Those great words, not yet spoken when Aubrey was born, might have been coined for him, and for us to remember him by as long as we ourselves are on earth.

Bibliography

Charterhouse Records 1850-1900 Edited by B. Ellis
Charterhouse A.H. Tod, G. Bell and Sons, 1919
Charterhouse Old and New E.P. Eardley Wilmot and E.C. Streatfield, 1895
Cambridge Daily News and various Brighton and Sussex newspapers
The Cambridge University Cricket Club W.J. Ford, (Blackwood & Sons, 1902)
Corinthians and Cricketers Edward Grayson (Sportsman's Book Club, 1957)
Famous Sussex Cricketers A.D. Taylor (Hove Gazette Printing and Publishing Co., 1898)
Sussex County Cricket 1728-1923 Alfred J. Gaston (Southern Publishing Co. Ltd., 1924)
Sussex Sir Home Gordon, Bt. (Convoy Publications, 1950)
Aubrey Smith's Scrapbooks (K.A. Auty Library, Ridley College, Canada)
The Visit of Major Warton's English Cricket Team to South Africa (Impey Walton & Co., 1888-1889)
The Cricketing Record of Major Warton's Tour, 1888-9 Charles Cox, 1889
Southern Africa, Today and Yesterday A. W. Wells (J.M. Dent & Sons, 1956)
Articles in *Cricket, Cricket Field, Wisden Cricket Monthly*, and the *Cricketer*
Life Worth Living C.B. Fry (Eyre and Spottiswoode, 1939)
A Yankee Looks at Cricket, as told to Gerald Brodribb by Henry Sayen, (Putnam, 1956)
Hollywood Cricket Club Scorebooks
46 Not Out Hollis and Carter, 1948
Crusoe on Cricket, with an introduction by Alan Ross A. Ross (1966)
The Cricket Addict's Archive Edited by Benny Green (Elm Tree Books, 1977)
Cricket and All That Denis Compton and Bill Edrich (Pelham Books, 1978)
Archie, A Biography of A.C. MacLaren Michael Down (George Allen & Unwin, 1981)
Honor Cobb's personal scrapbooks
Bernard Shaw Collected Plays with their Prefaces (Bodley Head, 1971)
Sir George Alexander and the St James' Theatre A.E.W. Mason (Macmillan & Co. 1935)
The Days I Knew The autobiography of Lillie Langtry (Collins, 1978)
Mrs Patrick Campbell Alan Dent (Museum Press Ltd, 1961)
The Truth About Pygmalion Richard Huggett (William Heinemann Ltd, 1969)

A Victorian Playgoer Kate Terry Gielgud (Heinemann, 1980)

Behind the Scenes with Cyril Maude by himself (John Murray, 1927)

With a feather on my nose Billie Burke (Peter Davies, 1950)

Showman William R. Brady (E.P. Dutton & Co., 1937)

The Barrymores Hollis Alpert (W.H. Allen, 1964)

Me - and the Stage Naomi Jacob (William Kimber, 1964)

To Tell My Story Irene Vanbrugh (Hutchinson & Co., 1948)

One Boy's War Richard Hough (Heinemann, 1975)

A Hundred Different Lives Raymond Massey (Robson Books, 1979)

The Loved One Evelyn Waugh (Penguin Books, 1948)

Bring on the Empty Horses David Niven (Hamish Hamilton, 1975)

Autobiography Cecil B. De Mille (W.H. Allen, 1960)

Picturegoer articles

Old English in Hollywood W.J. Makin

Sir Aubrey Smith: 84 Not Out Clarissa Churchill

The M.G.M. Story John Douglas Eames (Octopus Books, 1975)

A Biographical Dictionary of Film David Thomson (William Morrow & Co., 1976)

Halliwell's Filmgoers' Companion Leslie Halliwell (Granada Publishing, 1977)

Halliwell's Film Guide Leslie Halliwell (Granada Publishing, 1977)

The Hollywood Studios Roy Pickard (Frederick Muller Ltd, 1978)

Charmed Lives Michael Korda (Allen Lane, 1980)

Index